THE
ELIZABETH II
POCKET BIBLE

THE
POCKET BIBLE
SERIES

THE
ELIZABETH II
POCKET BIBLE

TERESA PADDINGTON

PB POCKET BIBLES

This edition first published in Great Britain 2012 by
Crimson Publishing, a division of Crimson Publishing Ltd
Westminster House
Kew Road
Richmond
Surrey
TW9 2ND

© Crimson Publishing Ltd, 2012

A catalogue record for this book is available from the British Library.

ISBN 978 1 907087 486

Typeset by IDSUK (DataConnection) Ltd
Printed and bound by Lego Print SpA, Trento

CONTENTS

ACKNOWLEDGEMENTS

I would like to thank Murray, the best cocker spaniel in the world, for keeping me sane while writing this book.

Thanks to Holly Ivins at Crimson Publishing for all her help and for always being on the end of the phone in times of trouble.

My biggest thanks go to the woman who this book is about. When I came to write this book, if you had asked me, I would have said that Queen Elizabeth is a good queen but it's not as though she has a proper job! After researching this book, if asked I will say that I am full of admiration for someone who could do this role for so long, with such dedication and always with a smile.

INTRODUCTION

'Most people have a job and then they go home. In this existence, job and life go on together because you can't really divide it up.'
Her Majesty, The Queen, Elizabeth II (1992)

The Queen is such a familiar part of our lives; we see her image every time we spend money or lick a stamp and we see photographs of her in our newspapers. But how much do we actually know about her?

This book will tell you all you need to know about the Queen's life, her interests and her family. Packed with lesser known and interesting facts and insightful quotes from people who have met and worked with her. The book will also tell you about the Queen's life, from where she was born, her childhood, her marriage and how a 10-year-old girl suddenly found herself next in line to the throne, and Queen at the age of just 25.

The role and powers of the monarchy have been eroded over time, and today it is sometimes difficult to understand their relevance in this modern age. This book will outline the powers the Queen has today and how she still fulfils two very important roles as Head of State and Head of the Nation.

The Queen could not carry out these duties without the help of the Royal Family and the royal household. In this book you will find profiles of members of the Royal Family. It will also take you inside the royal household and describe how this well-oiled machine organises the Queen's official duties and will tell you who is responsible for the day-to-day running of 'the Firm'.

Throughout the year the Queen attends a number of royal events that are full of colour, tradition, pomp and circumstance. This book details these events and where and when they take place.

It is important for the Queen to look like a queen when attending these events, and although her style has changed over the years she still stands out in a crowd, whether dressed in a lovely gown with her crown or more informally with her trademark hats and handbag. This book will describe a few of the more outstanding outfits as well as detailing some of the stunning Crown jewels and the Queen's private collection.

We'll also look at what it means to be the Queen, from having your image on currency and stamps, to the films and television programmes made about her life, as well as describing the 'real' Queen and some of her hobbies.

From the day of Queen Elizabeth's coronation over 60 years ago, her life has been dedicated to serving the country and her people. Despite the number of hands she has shaken and people whom she has spoken to during her reign, the oath she took on the day of her coronation is still as strong today:

'I have in sincerity pledged myself to your service, as so many of you are pledged to mine. Throughout all my life and with all my heart I shall strive to be worthy of your trust.'

BIOGRAPHY

Over the past 60 years no other woman has had so much written about her life. This chapter will highlight and bring together some of the significant moments of the Queen's life as well as giving insight into the real Queen, her hobbies, and her interests when she is not representing the longest reigning monarchy in the world.

♔ BIRTH ♔

Queen Elizabeth II was born on 21 April 1926 at 2.40am at 17 Bruton Street, Mayfair, London, the home of her maternal grandparents, the Earl and Countess of Strathmore. The birth of Elizabeth is commemorated by a plaque on the wall of the office block that replaced 17 Bruton Street in 1937.

Pocket fact 🎗

During her labour, the Duchess of York was attended by the then Home Secretary Sir William Joynson-Hicks, to ensure that there was no baby-swapping. The custom came from the accusation that in 1688, Mary Modena, the wife of James II, smuggled a changeling in a warming pan.

The birth of the future queen was greeted with much joy by the public, who were suffering from the economic deprivation of the 1920s and so were glad to have something to celebrate. The baby was christened Elizabeth, after her mother, Alexandra after her paternal great-grandmother Queen Alexandra, and Mary after her maternal grandmother Queen Mary, in the private chapel in Buckingham Palace on 29 May 1926.

Elizabeth was christened in the silver gilt lily font (which can be seen in the Jewel House at the Tower of London). The font was commissioned by Queen Victoria in 1840 because she did not want her children christened in the same font as the illegitimate children of King Charles II. The font has been used for every royal christening since then with the exception of Princess Beatrice (who was christened at Sandringham).

♔ A RELATIVELY ORDINARY ♔ FAMILY LIFE

Because Elizabeth was the daughter of the second son of George V there was very little likelihood of her inheriting the throne. This meant that her home life was relatively ordinary for the daughter of a duke.

The family originally lived in White Lodge in Richmond Park (now the home of the Royal Ballet School) and when Elizabeth was one year old, the family moved to an elegant 25-bedroom 18th-century town house at 145 Piccadilly. As befitting her father's status and in accordance with the lifestyle of the aristocracy in the 1920s, Elizabeth had a suite of nursery rooms supervised by her nanny Clara Cooper Knight and her nursery maid Margaret Macdonald, affectionately known as 'Bobo', as this was the first word Elizabeth spoke.

Pocket fact 🎀

Bobo went on to become Elizabeth's dresser and remained in her service for 67 years. When Bobo died in 1993 at the age of 89, she had become Elizabeth's closest confidante, daily companion and one of the very few people outside the family to call her 'Lilibet'. It is believed that Elizabeth took Bobo a cup of tea in bed on her birthday every year.

A BABY SISTER

Elizabeth became a big sister when Princess Margaret was born in 1930. Although there was four years between Elizabeth and Margaret they were very close, especially as their parents often were away on official royal duties. Contemporary accounts described Elizabeth as thoughtful, happy, intelligent and poised, and Margaret as playful and the joker of the family.

Unlike many royal and aristocratic families, the Duke and Duchess of York were very hands-on parents for the times, spending time with their children whenever they were not travelling on official trips. They liked to bathe their daughters, play with them and read to them. It was not unusual for the family to gather around the piano for a sing-song.

The Duke of York was also a keen amateur photographer and there are many touching pictures taken by him, just like any proud parent, of his daughter Elizabeth, with her blonde curls, piercing blue eyes and smiling face. When the Duke and Duchess undertook a six-month overseas tour to Australia and New Zealand, in early 1927 they were kept up to date with their young daughter's progress with regular photographs.

Pocket fact 🎴

The young Elizabeth had difficulty in pronouncing her own name, calling herself 'Lilibet' instead. This became the family name for Elizabeth.

♛ THE DUKE OF YORK ♛
BECOMES GEORGE VI

Given the extraordinary pressures of becoming a king, it was normal for the eldest son to be prepared from a young age for the responsibility. Thus, Elizabeth's uncle Edward had been groomed for the throne, and when he decided to abdicate in 1936 it came as a shock not only for the nation but also for his shy and quiet brother. The Duke of York had a speech impediment and had not been prepared for the role now thrust upon him.

Edward VIII had been courting the twice-divorced American Wallis Simpson and wanted to marry her, but as head of the Church of England, which did not recognise divorce, this was not possible. On 11 December 1936 Edward VIII broadcast to the nation announcing his decision to abdicate saying that he 'found the burden of heavy responsibility too great to bear' without the support of the woman he loved.

Pocket fact 🎫

King Edward VIII is the only British monarch to have abdicated the throne.

Elizabeth's father the Duke was happiest mixing with ordinary people out of the limelight, and had attended Dartmouth Naval College in 1909 and joined the navy as a midshipman in 1913. In 1916 he sailed on the HMS *Collingwood* and took part in the Battle of Jutland, one of the largest sea battles in naval war history. He was popular with his men and was mentioned in despatches.

Royal remarks 🐕

It is said that when Edward was signing the Instrument of Abdication, the Duke of York turned to his cousin Louis Mountbatten and said: 'I never wanted this to happen. I am quite unprepared for it. David [Edward] has been trained for this all his life.'

Although christened Albert, the Duke of York was crowned King George VI on 12 May 1937, in honour of his father and to create a sense of continuity of the monarchy. As soon as the abdication had been announced the quiet family life enjoyed by the Duke and

Duchess of York ended. They moved to Buckingham Palace and 10-year-old Elizabeth became the next in line to the throne.

Pocket fact 🎖

As the eldest daughter of the monarch, Elizabeth's title was Heir Presumptive and not Heir Apparent. Elizabeth's right to become the next monarch was because her father did not have a son and she was the eldest child. If George had had a son, even though he would be younger than Elizabeth, he would have become the heir apparent.

♛ EDUCATION ♛

Elizabeth did not go to school but was educated at home by her governess Marion Crawford, 'Crawfie', who taught her history, arithmetic, geography, grammar, literature and writing. When her father became King and Elizabeth the Heir Presumptive, Elizabeth's education was increased to include lessons in the role of monarch from her father plus constitutional history and law, taught by the Vice-Provost of Eton College. She was also taught religious studies and canon law by the Archbishop of Canterbury (Cosmo Gordon Lang).

Elizabeth and Margaret were taught French from Mrs Montaudon-Smith, 'Monty', and Vicomtesse de Bellaigue. Elizabeth studied art and music and learned to swim at the London Bath Club in Dover Street (now closed).

Pocket fact 🎖

It was at the Bath Club that Elizabeth won the over-9 and under-14 Children's Challenge Shield and Margaret the under-9 Challenge Cup. The cups were for swimming one length of the pool in backstroke, breaststroke, one dive and a life-saving demonstration.

The King and Queen had just come back from an official visit to America and one of the first events they attended was their daughter's swimming competition where the Queen awarded the prizes.

♛ ROYAL GIRL GUIDES ♛

Elizabeth's nurse Marion Crawford started a Girl Guide Company to give Elizabeth and Margaret more opportunity to mix with girls of their own age. In 1937, the Buckingham Palace Guide Company, known as the 1st Buckingham Palace, was formed with 20 Girl Guides drawn from cousins, friends and palace employees. A Brownie Pack was also created for Margaret, made up of 14 girls, as she was only seven and therefore too young to join the Girl Guides.

> *Pocket fact* 🎟
>
> *Elizabeth was elected at the first meeting as second in command in the Kingfisher patrol, while her cousin Patricia Mountbatten was elected as leader.*

The Girl Guides met in the summer house in the garden of Buckingham Palace and used Windsor Forest for trekking, bird watching and camp fires. When Elizabeth finished Girl Guides in 1943 she enrolled as a Sea Ranger on *SRS President III* and in 1945 became a Sea Ranger Commodore.

> *Pocket fact* 🎟
>
> *Some of the badges gained by Elizabeth as a Girl Guide were for cook, child nurse, needlewoman and interpreter.*

♛ ROYAL DUTIES AT A ♛ YOUNG AGE

The most important part of Elizabeth's education as Heir Presumptive came from watching and taking part in official duties with her parents and her grandmother, Queen Mary. Even before her father became king, Elizabeth was used to being in the public eye. From a very early age she was expected to behave with dignity and decorum. The media interest in the Royal Family is not a 21st-century obsession, and crowds would gather outside 145 Piccadilly to watch her and Margaret play. When Elizabeth wore a particular colour as a baby it then became the fashion.

Royal remarks 🐕

Winston Churchill met Elizabeth when she was just two years old and he noted that 'she had an air of authority and reflectiveness astonishing in an infant'.

In 1929, aged three, Elizabeth appeared on the cover of *Time* magazine and in May 1930 aged just four she attended the Naval and Military Tournament at Olympia with her grandmother Queen Mary. Elizabeth saw how her grandmother, father and mother dealt with the public and the constant media attention. Although a shy man, her father set his daughter an example of duty and responsibility that was to stay with her for the rest of her life. Her mother's charm and way of engaging with the public endeared her to the British people during the Second World War and beyond, and could not have set Elizabeth a better example.

Pocket fact 🎟

With the popularity of cinema growing in the early part of the 20th century, the Royal Family's private and public life was shown on newsreels all over the world as never before.

♛ GEORGE VI'S CORONATION ♛

George VI's coronation took place in 1937 when Elizabeth was 11 years of age. The pomp and ceremony of the coronation and Westminster Abbey crowded with thousands of people, all dressed in their finery, would have been overwhelming for an adult let alone an 11-year-old girl.

Royal remarks 🐕

Elizabeth and Margaret were not excluded from the ceremony and even though Elizabeth was used to grand occasions, the sight of the abbey on the day of the coronation impressed the young princess as she describes Westminster Abbey in an essay she wrote for her parents: 'The arches and beams at the top were covered in a sort of haze of wonder as Papa was crowned; at least I thought it was.'

On the newsreel pictures of the coronation it looks as if her grandmother Queen Mary is explaining the service to her granddaughter, but the essay Elizabeth wrote about the coronation reveals that they were counting the pages to the end of the service because 'it had got rather boring as it was all prayers'.

After the coronation, the Royal Family appeared on the balcony of Buckingham Palace with thousands of people lining the Mall leading up to the palace.

Elizabeth continued to accompany her parents on official visits and in 1938 at a National Service at Windsor she watched a march-past by Girl Guides dressed in her own Girl Guide uniform.

♛ THE SECOND WORLD WAR ♛

Following the outbreak of the Second World War in 1940, at the age of 14 Elizabeth made her first live broadcast on radio on the BBC's children's programme to all the children of Great Britain and the Commonwealth. The broadcast was particularly for the children being evacuated due to the danger of German bombing. Elizabeth spoke of:

'feeling so much for you as we know what it means to be away from those we love most of all'.

Whether this referred to being separated from her parents during the war, as Elizabeth and Margaret were sent to Windsor Castle, or when her parents were away on official duties, is unclear.

It was suggested that Elizabeth and Margaret should be sent to Canada for safety but their mother Queen Elizabeth said: 'The children won't go without me. I won't leave without the King and the King will never leave.'

Pocket fact 🚩

During the Second World War, Elizabeth had to carry an identity card and a ration book just like any other British subject. Ration books contained coupons which shopkeepers cut out or crossed through when customers paid for rationed items such as food and clothing. Elizabeth's ration books survived the war and have been preserved in the Royal Archives at Windsor Castle.

WORK AND THE BEGINNING OF OFFICIAL DUTIES

On 25 April 1942, just four days after her 16th birthday Elizabeth registered at the Windsor Labour Exchange, as the law stated that all girls over the age of 16 were expected to work (Elizabeth was not expected to undertake any work but she still had to register). In 1943, Elizabeth carried out her first official solo duty when she spent the day with a grenadier tank battalion.

Pocket fact 🔲

It wasn't all official duties for Elizabeth from 1941 to 1944. Christmas pantomimes were regularly performed in the Waterloo Chamber in Windsor Castle for the Royal Family, servants and pupils from the Royal School at Windsor. In 1943, Elizabeth and Margaret took part in Aladdin *and in 1944 in* Old Mother Red Riding Boots.

Elizabeth's life as patron of many charities now began in earnest. She was particularly interested in organisations that involved young people and she was made president of the Queen Elizabeth Hospital for Children in Hackney and the National Society for the Prevention of Cruelty to Children.

During the war everyone in Britain was expected to plant food in every spare acre of land and the Royal Family did their bit too. In 1943 the news showed Elizabeth and the King, Queen and Margaret riding around the Sandringham House estate on bicycles inspecting the harvest of corn, oats and rye from the fields that had replaced the golf course and lawns.

In 1944 whilst her father was touring the Italian battlefields, Elizabeth was appointed Counsellor of State. During this time Elizabeth carried out some of the duties of a head of state such as receiving an address from the House of Commons and replying on behalf of the throne. In September 1944, Elizabeth accompanied her parents on her first official tour of Scotland and undertook her first official opening ceremony – of the Aberdeen Sailors' Home.

Pocket fact 🔲

The Counsellor of State is appointed from one of five members of the Royal Family, to temporarily carry out some of the sovereign's duties in their absence, due to sickness or a trip abroad. The current counsellors are the Duke of Edinburgh, Prince Charles, Prince William, Prince Harry and the Duke of York.

LIFE IN THE MILITARY

Elizabeth was keen to get into one of the military services and in February 1945, aged 18, she joined the Auxiliary Territorial Service (ATS) as No. 230973 Second Subaltern Elizabeth Alexandra Mary Windsor, 5 feet 3 inches, eyes blue and hair brown. The new recruits were sent to army camps for basic training, where at the end of four weeks they completed written and practical tests to see which job they were suited for.

Pocket fact 🖋

In October 2003, at an exhibition in the Imperial War Museum to commemorate the efforts of British Women in wartime, Elizabeth was reunited with six former members of the ATS. One of the women remembered that during training Elizabeth 'found it very strange to be working with a lot of people. I'm quite certain that's why she sent her daughter to a public school because she enjoyed being with others.'

Elizabeth trained as a driver and motor mechanic. The many pictures of the young and attractive Princess Elizabeth in uniform, with a greasy spanner in hand and her head stuck under the bonnet of a lorry was an enormous boost for recruitment into the ATS. The King and Queen came to watch their daughter fixing an engine, and when they returned back to her after visiting the other areas of the camp, the King joked with her saying 'haven't you got it mended yet?' By the end of the war she had been promoted to junior commander and had passed out as a fully qualified driver.

Pocket fact 🖋

Because she trained as a driver in the ATS, Elizabeth is the only monarch to have held a proper driving licence. Although all members of the Royal Family have to take a driving test it is not a legal requirement for them to have a licence.

END OF THE SECOND WORLD WAR

On Victory in Europe Day on 8 May 1945, as the crowds packed the Mall, Elizabeth appeared once again on the balcony of Buckingham Palace, this time dressed in her ATS uniform, with the King, Queen, Margaret and Winston Churchill to celebrate the end of the Second World War.

Royal remarks

Elizabeth and Margaret left Buckingham Palace to mingle with the celebrating crowds. Elizabeth said: 'We asked my parents if we could go out and see for ourselves . . . I remember lines of unknown people linking arms and walking down Whitehall, all of us were just swept along on a tide of happiness and relief.'

Now that the war had ended, Elizabeth's official duties as heir to the throne began in earnest. In 1947 Elizabeth accompanied the King, Queen and Margaret on her first official overseas tour to South Africa. It was from Cape Town on her 21st birthday that Elizabeth made a radio broadcast where she pledged to the Commonwealth:

'I declare before you all that my whole life, whether long or short, shall be devoted to your service and the service of our great imperial family to which we all belong.'

♚ COURTSHIP AND MARRIAGE ♚

COURTSHIP

Elizabeth and Philip had known each other since childhood because of their close family connection; Elizabeth is Philip's third cousin through Queen Victoria and the son of Prince Andrew of Greece. Therefore it was inevitable that their paths would cross, which they first did at the wedding of the Duke of Kent in 1934. Elizabeth was eight years old, and a bridesmaid at her uncle's wedding, while Philip was 12.

In 1939 Philip enrolled as a cadet at the Britannia Royal Naval College in Dartmouth, Devon. The Royal Family had decided to take the Royal Yacht *Victoria and Albert* on a short trip, calling in at Dartmouth where the King had been a naval cadet. Because of his relationship with the Royal Family, Philip was asked to dine on the Royal Yacht and spent time over the weekend playing games with the young princesses. According to many reports it was love at first sight for the 13-year-old Elizabeth.

Royal remarks 🐕

In a documentary to celebrate Prince Philip's 90th birthday, Lady Mountbatten describes Elizabeth's feelings saying, 'I think early on she was quite smitten, quite early on, when they first met. Of course his background was not very different at all from the Queen's background so he wasn't overawed or worried by it.'

During the war years Philip continued to serve in the Royal Navy. In 1941 he saw action on HMS *Valiant*, was mentioned in despatches and later awarded the Greek Cross of Valour.

The couple corresponded while he was away, and when Philip was in Britain he would call in for a meal. He spent Christmas at Windsor Castle in 1943, sitting in the front row to watch that year's performance of *Aladdin* starring Elizabeth as Aladdin.

In 1946 Philip visited Balmoral Castle (the Royal Family's private Scottish home) and proposed to Elizabeth and was accepted. Elizabeth's father felt that at 20 she was too young for a formal engagement and persuaded the couple to wait until after Elizabeth's 21st birthday to be formally engaged.

Pocket fact 🔲

Prince Philip's Greek nationality would have been a stumbling block to the engagement, but he had become a British subject in 1947 and changed his name to Philip Mountbatten, an anglicised version of his maternal grandfather's name Battenberg.

Elizabeth and Philip announced their engagement on 10 July 1947. The engagement ring was made of platinum with a large three-carat, square-cut diamond and five smaller diamonds on the side. It was designed by Philip. The diamonds for Elizabeth's engagement ring were taken from a tiara owned by Philip's mother Princess Alice.

Prior to the wedding George VI appointed Elizabeth a Knight of the Garter (the highest order of chivalry in Britain that dates back to 1348) and bestowed the title of His Royal Highness, the Duke of Edinburgh on Philip. George appointed Philip the Duke of Edinburgh a week later so that Elizabeth had seniority.

THE WEDDING

The wedding took place at Westminster Abbey on 20 November 1947 and there was much discussion as to how lavish it should be, given that the country was still experiencing rationing and still bore the scars of the Second World War. Prince Philip was against a lavish occasion but many felt that a return to the pageantry of a royal occasion was just what the country needed.

Pocket fact 🔲

One newspaper polled its readers to see which they would prefer and 86% of the readers voted for 'the traditional gaiety of a gala public event'.

Thousands of people turned out to watch the pageantry and colour of a royal occasion, the first they had seen since the end of the war and in some instances the watching crowd were 50 deep. After the ceremony, Elizabeth and Philip made the traditional appearance on the balcony of Buckingham Palace to the crowds waiting in the Mall. After her marriage Elizabeth became known also as the Duchess of Edinburgh.

The dress

Elizabeth's ivory silk wedding dress was designed by her mother's favourite designer Norman Hartnell. It was decorated with crystals and 10,000 pearls and had a 15-foot, star-patterned train. Clothing was still rationed even for a princess and Elizabeth had to collect the 3,000 clothing coupons needed for the material for her dress. Many people donated clothing coupons to Elizabeth to help with the wedding dress but they had to be sent back as it was illegal to give them away.

The tulle veil took seven weeks to make and was held in place by a diamond fringe tiara loaned to Elizabeth by her grandmother Queen Mary.

The bouquet

Elizabeth's bouquet contained white orchids and included a sprig of myrtle from a tree grown from a sprig in the bouquet of Queen Victoria at Osborne House, the old home of Queen Victoria. A sprig of myrtle from this tree has been included in every royal bride's bouquet since 1850 including Catherine's, the Duchess of Cambridge, in 2011.

The wedding presents

Elizabeth and Philip received over 2,500 wedding presents, including a Royal Worcester dinner and dessert service, 500 tins of pineapple for distribution by the bride, an electric washing machine, a refrigerator, a Singer sewing machine and, from the Girl Guides of Australia, dried fruit to make a wedding cake.

Top ten facts about the Royal Wedding

1. Elizabeth sent her wedding bouquet back to Westminster Abbey to be put on the Tomb of the Unknown Soldier as have all subsequent royal brides.

2. The kneelers used by Elizabeth and Philip were made from orange boxes due to wartime shortages and were covered in pink silk.

3. Elizabeth's wedding ring was made from Welsh gold. The same gold mine also made the wedding rings of Elizabeth's mother, Diana, Princess of Wales and Catherine, Duchess of Cambridge.

4. The official wedding cake was made by McVities and Price. McVities also made Prince William's favourite cake for his wedding in 2011 from a secret recipe of rich tea biscuits and chocolate.

5. When Elizabeth was ready, no one could find the bouquet until a footman finally remembered he had put it in a cool room to keep it fresh.

6. Elizabeth's diamond tiara broke as it was placed on her head and a quick repair had to be made.

7. The pearls Elizabeth had planned to wear, a gift from her parents, ended up on display with the rest of the wedding gifts in St James's Palace and her private secretary had to rush to retrieve them.

8. On the morning of the wedding, Philip ordered tea and coffee to be served to the photographers waiting outside in the cold.

9. The couple left for their honeymoon at Broadlands in Hampshire with Elizabeth's favourite dog, a corgi called Susan.

10. In 2007 the couple celebrated their 60th diamond wedding anniversary at Westminster Abbey with family and friends, as well as 10 other couples who were also married on the 20 November 1947.

♔ ELIZABETH BECOMES QUEEN ♔

From 1949 to 1951 Elizabeth divided her time between Malta, where Philip was serving in the Royal Navy, and Britain. This idyllic lifestyle came to an end when the health of her father deteriorated. George had been unwell for some time with lung cancer and Elizabeth had taken on more and more of his official duties, touring Canada and the US in October 1951. When George waved goodbye to his daughter Elizabeth as she left for her official Commonwealth tour on 1 February 1952, it was the last time they saw each other. Just a few days later on 6 February 1952 Elizabeth became Queen Elizabeth II when her father George VI died of a heart attack aged 56.

When the news of her father's death reached the 25-year-old Elizabeth, she was staying at Tree Tops, Sagana Lodge, Kenya. The news took several hours to reach where they were staying and it was Philip who broke the news of her beloved father's death. The tour was stopped and Elizabeth immediately returned to London. She was greeted on arrival by ministers of her government, including Prime Minister Winston Churchill. It was just one week since her father had waved her goodbye from the very spot she was now returning to as queen.

Pocket fact 🎟

The Queen descended the steps of the plane dressed in a black coat and hat, which had been packed just in case the worst should happen.

THE ACCESSION

Elizabeth automatically became queen on the death of her father. She was thus immediately proclaimed Queen at the Accession Council in St James's Palace on 6 February. The proclamation was then read out at Charing Cross, Temple Bar and the Royal Exchange in the City of London, Edinburgh, Windsor and York, and at shire halls and guildhalls throughout the country and throughout the Commonwealth nations.

Pocket fact 🖪

The Accession Council is made up of all members of the Privy Council who advise the sovereign on the exercise of the Royal Prerogative, her personal powers, and carry them out on her behalf. The Lord Mayor and aldermen of the City of London and high commissioners of Commonwealth realm countries are invited to attend.

On 8 February the Queen attended St James's Palace and read out the Accession Declaration, which contained the following words in recognition of her father's work:

> *'By the sudden death of my dear father I am called to assume the duties and responsibilities of sovereignty. My heart is too full for me to say more to you today than I shall always work, as my father did throughout his reign, to advance the happiness and prosperity of my peoples, spread as they are all the world over.'*

Royal remarks 🐕

The Queen told a friend not long after the Accession that she 'no longer felt anxious or worried. I don't know what it is — but I have lost my timidity somehow becoming the Sovereign and having to receive the prime minister'.

♔ THE CORONATION ♔

On 2 June 1953, after 16 months of planning, the day of Elizabeth's coronation arrived. The Queen would now go through the same service she had watched her father go through 16 years earlier. Street parties were organised, flags hung from lamp posts and the nation got ready to party after the austerity of the war years. For the first time the coronation was to be televised with the permission of the Queen.

Pocket fact 🎞

Twenty-seven million people watched the coronation on television. Many had bought a television just to watch the event and invited friends and neighbours without televisions to watch theirs. For many it was the first time they had ever watched an event on television.

The miserable rainy day did not stop three million people from lining the streets, some of them sleeping on the streets for two nights, to cheer for their new queen. Stands were built in various locations including opposite Westminster Abbey to allow people to get a better view of the wonderful procession and the young Queen.

The coronation service began at 11.15am and lasted for three hours (see p.81 for more details). At the end of the service the Queen left the Abbey to the sound of the cheering crowds and drove in the Gold State Coach with Prince Philip to appear on the balcony of Buckingham Palace with the Royal Family.

Pocket fact 🎞

The Queen's actual birthday is on 21 April but her official birthday (the date of her coronation) is not a fixed date. It falls on the first, second or third Saturday in June and is decided by the government every year.

♔ BIRTH OF THE QUEEN'S ♔ CHILDREN

The Queen has four children: Prince Charles, Princess Anne, Prince Andrew and Prince Edward.

PRINCE CHARLES

Prince Charles, the heir to the throne, was born to Princess Elizabeth at Buckingham Palace on 14 November 1948 and weighed 7lbs 6oz.

The announcement posted on the gates of Buckingham Palace said 'Her Royal Highness the Princess Elizabeth, the Duchess of Edinburgh, was safely delivered of a Prince at 9.14pm this evening. Her Royal Highness and the infant Prince are both doing well'. There were around 3,000 people waiting outside Buckingham Palace for news of the impending birth and a rousing chorus of 'For he's a jolly good fellow' broke out.

Royal remarks 🐕

On 1 December, just two weeks after the birth, the Queen wrote to her second cousin Lady Mary Cambridge saying: 'The baby is very sweet, and Philip and I are enormously proud of him. I still find it hard to believe that I really have a baby of my own!'

Prince Charles was christened Charles Philip Arthur George on 15 December 1948 in the Music Room at Buckingham Palace. The christening photographs show four generations of the Windsors: Prince Charles, his great-grandmother Queen Mary, his grandparents King George VI and Queen Elizabeth, and his mother Princess Elizabeth.

Pocket fact 🗝

The christening robe Charles wore was first worn by Princess Victoria, the eldest daughter of Queen Victoria in 1847. The robe was worn by every royal baby since, but in 2008 an exact replica was used for the first time at the christening of the Earl of Wessex's son Viscount Severn, as the original robe is now preserved in a special container.

PRINCESS ANNE

Princess Anne was born at 11.50am on 15 August 1950 at Clarence House and weighed 6lbs. The announcement of her birth was posted outside Clarence House, and, as had been done with Prince Charles's birth, programmes were interrupted in the USA to announce the birth. In Australia audiences in theatres and cinemas cheered when news of the birth was broadcast.

Princess Anne was christened Anne Elizabeth Alice Louise in the Music Room at Buckingham Palace on 21 October 1950 by the Archbishop of York. There was considerable interest in the new baby, and a month after the birth, when Elizabeth left London for Balmoral, crowds of people waited outside Clarence House and at King's Cross Station to catch a glimpse of the new princess.

Pocket fact 🛈

After the Duke had signed Princess Anne's birth certificate at Buckingham Palace he was given her identity card, ration book (rationing after the war was still in place) and bottles of cod liver oil and orange juice.

PRINCE ANDREW

Prince Andrew was named after his paternal grandfather Prince Andrew of Greece and was born on 19 February 1960 at Buckingham Palace. He was christened Andrew Albert Christian Edward in the Music Room in Buckingham Palace on 8 April 1960.

Pocket fact 🛈

Prince Andrew was the first child to be born to a reigning monarch for over a century, the first since Queen Victoria's daughter Princess Beatrice.

PRINCE EDWARD

Prince Edward is the youngest child of the Queen and was born on 10 March 1964 at Buckingham Palace. He was christened Edward Anthony Richard Louis at Windsor Castle on 2 May 1964.

Pocket fact 🛡

Prince Edward's first public appearance was in June 1964 on the balcony of Buckingham Palace after the Trooping the Colour.

♔ THE QUEEN'S JUBILEES ♔

THE SILVER JUBILEE

In 1977 the Queen celebrated the 25th anniversary of her accession to the throne. Celebrations took place throughout the country and the Commonwealth. The actual anniversary was on 6 February but as the weather is not good at that time of the year, the full celebrations did not take place until the summer. The Queen decided that she wanted to meet as many people as possible both at home and overseas.

Top ten facts about the Silver Jubilee

1. *In the space of three months the Queen embarked on six jubilee tours visiting 36 of the 86 counties in the UK.*
2. *In this jubilee year the Queen and Prince Philip travelled over 56,000 miles.*
3. *Official overseas visits were made to Commonwealth countries including Western Samoa, Australia, New Zealand, Tonga, Papua New Guinea, Canada and the West Indies.*
4. *On 6 June the Queen lit a beacon at Windsor Castle, which was the signal for a series of beacons to be lit across the country.*

5. On 7 June the Queen and Prince Philip travelled to St Paul's Cathedral in the Gold State Coach for a Service of Thanksgiving.

6. Also on 7 June at a lunch at the Guildhall the Queen gave a speech in which she said: 'My Lord Mayor, when I was 21 I pledged my life to the service of our people and I asked for God's help to make good that vow. Although that vow was made in my salad days, when I was green in judgement, I do not regret nor retract one word of it.'

7. The procession back to Buckingham Palace from the Guildhall was watched by 500 million people throughout the country and the Commonwealth.

8. On 9 June the Queen travelled down the River Thames from Greenwich to Lambeth.

9. The Queen opened the South Bank Jubilee Gardens and Silver Jubilee Walkway which connects some of London's most iconic landmarks including Buckingham Palace and St Paul's Cathedral.

10. The day ended with a firework display, with the Queen returning to Buckingham Palace for the traditional balcony appearance before a cheering crowd.

THE GOLDEN JUBILEE

In 2002 the Queen celebrated the 50th anniversary of her accession to the throne. The Queen's Golden Jubilee was a well-organised event, coordinated by the Golden Jubilee Office, part of the Department for Culture, Media and Sport. The jubilee had six themes: celebration, community, service, past and future, giving thanks and commonwealth. The Queen had a programme of events that included travelling the length and breadth of the country and visiting Commonwealth countries. On 4 June hundreds of thousands of people turned out to watch the Queen travel to St Paul's Cathedral in a ceremonial procession for a National Service of Thanksgiving. The Queen then appeared on the balcony of Buckingham Palace to greet the crowds who had congregated on the Mall.

Top ten facts about the Golden Jubilee

1. There were 28 million hits on the Golden Jubilee website and the Queen sent two emails, one from Norwich to all schools in Norfolk, and the other from Wells to schools around the world. She received 30,000 emails.

2. The Queen received over 600 gifts including knitted toys, fruit trees, tea cosies, china corgis and portraits.

3. The Empire State Building was lit in purple and gold lights on the evening of 4 June 2002 in honour of the Queen's jubilee.

4. Street parties were held all over the world including in the Antarctic, where 20 scientists held the coldest party at -20°C.

5. Three special garden parties were held: one for a selection of people who were born on the day of the Queen's accession on 6 February 1952; the second was the Party at the Palace, which was a pop concert with artists including Paul McCartney, Elton John, Tony Bennett and Brian May of the group Queen, who played God Save the Queen on the roof of Buckingham Palace; the third was the Proms at the Palace which was a classical concert with artists including the famous opera singers Angela Gheorghiu and Roberto Alagna.

6. The Queen received a gold disc from the recording industry for the CD of Party at the Palace which sold 100,000 copies in the first week of its release.

7. Only a few monarchs have reached 50 years as monarch: Henry III, Edward III, James I, George III and Victoria.

8. The Queen flew around the world beginning with a visit to Jamaica on 18 February and then to New Zealand and Australia culminating with a trip to Canada in October.

9. *The Queen travelled the length and breadth of the UK, visiting 70 cities and towns in 38 days.*
10. *On 4 June the Queen and Prince Philip attended a Service of Thanksgiving at St Paul's Cathedral and returned to Buckingham Palace to attend the Golden Jubilee Festival in the Mall. They also made the traditional balcony appearance and watched a Royal Air Force (RAF) fly-past.*

DIAMOND JUBILEE

2012 marks 60 years since the Queen's accession. The main celebrations for the Queen's Diamond Jubilee will take place from Saturday 2 June to Tuesday 5 June 2012. The spring bank holiday will be moved to allow everyone to take part. Buckingham Palace is coordinating the celebrations, and for more details visit the official website of the British monarchy (www.royal.gov.uk).

Top ten facts about the Diamond Jubilee celebrations

1. *Buckingham Palace will be holding a concert, which will be televised by the BBC.*
2. *The Royal Commonwealth Society is organising a time capsule containing a digital archive of the Queen's reign. People from the UK and Commonwealth countries can choose a day of her reign and write about an event that is important to you, your family, community or country. For more details visit the society's website (www.thercs.org/society/jtc).*
3. *Greenwich is to be granted Royal Borough status, which will allow it to be called the Royal Borough of Greenwich in recognition of its historical ties with the monarchy.*
4. *St Paul's Cathedral will play host to the National Service of Thanksgiving.*

5. *Katherine Dewar won a competition promoted by the children's programme* Blue Peter *to design the official emblem for the Diamond Jubilee and she met the Queen at Buckingham Palace. The emblem is very colourful in red, blue, gold and white, with a Union Jack, and a crown on the top with the number 60 in the crown.*

6. *The Woodland Trust is to create a 460-acre public wood in Leicestershire and plant six million trees; 60 'diamond woods' will be created one for each year of the Queen's reign.*

7. *The 'Big Jubilee Lunch' will take place on 3 June 2012.*

8. *Thousands of beacons will be lit around the country on 4 June 2012, including 60 beacons on Hadrian's Wall, one for each year of the Queen's reign.*

9. *The Thames Diamond Jubilee Pageant will take place on 3 June 2012 when 1,000 boats led by the Queen in the Royal Barge will travel down the Thames.*

10. *At the summer opening of Buckingham Palace there will be a special exhibition of the Queen's diamonds.*

♔ THE QUEEN'S LIKES ♔ AND DISLIKES

The Queen **likes** to:

- drive herself around Balmoral and Sandringham

- leave up the Christmas decorations at Sandringham (where the family spend Christmas) until they leave in February

- take part in Scottish Country Dancing. The Queen is known to dance with the staff at the annual Gillies' Ball at Balmoral (a gillie is a man who advises or assists when fishing, fly fishing, deer stalking or hunting in Scotland)

- open personal mail herself – letters from family and friends have coded initials on the envelope

- keep the gold mirrored compact Prince Philip gave her on their wedding day in her handbag.

The Queen **dislikes**:

- long rambling speeches; people are warned to keep speeches short when the Queen attends official events

- tennis. The Queen only went to Wimbledon for her jubilee year in 1977

- sailing – although Prince Philip and Princess Anne are both skilled sailors

- wearing a seatbelt in the car

- duvets – she prefers sheets and blankets.

2

THE ROYAL FAMILY

The Royal Family is a group of close relatives who represent the British monarchy. They affectionately refer to themselves as 'the Firm' as they see themselves as a family business. The Royal Family supports the Queen in her official duties and will often attend events in her place if she is unable to attend. The family are patrons of various charities and organisations that interest them, giving freely of their time and bringing in additional revenue and public attention to these charities and organisations.

♔ FATHER: GEORGE VI ♔

(14 December 1895–6 February 1952)

George VI was christened Albert Frederick Arthur George and was known as Bertie by his family (when he became king he took the name of George in memory of his father). George was a shy child and suffered from knock knees meaning he was made to wear painful splints to straighten his legs. George battled with a bad stammer but as he was the second son this was not of too much concern. However, when his brother abdicated in 1936 (see p.3) it became a major problem because, as King, George VI would have to speak often in public. With the help of a speech therapist he eventually learnt to overcome his stammer.

Pocket fact 🚩

The film The King's Speech *(2010) starring Colin Firth gives an excellent portrayal of King George VI and the speech impediment he overcame.*

In 1920 George met Lady Elizabeth Bowes-Lyon and it is said that for George it was love at first sight. George married Lady Elizabeth Bowes-Lyon on 26 April 1923 after Elizabeth had refused his proposals twice. George VI's greatest achievements came about during the Second World War. The King seemed to instinctively know the right thing to do, visiting the bombed areas of the country and visiting the troops wherever and whenever possible. He went to North Africa after the victory of El Alamein in 1943 and in June 1944 he visited his army on the Normandy beaches just 10 days after the D-Day landings. George passed on to his daughter Elizabeth a great sense of duty, religious belief and responsibility. George VI died on 6 February 1952 at the age of 56.

Pocket fact 🛡

George VI was very conscious of the civilian contribution during the Second World War and introduced the George Cross and George Medal for civilian bravery and for military bravery when not engaged with the enemy.

♛ MOTHER: QUEEN ELIZABETH, ♛ THE QUEEN MOTHER

(4 August 1900–30 March 2002)

Lady Elizabeth Angela Marguerite Bowes-Lyon was the fourth daughter and ninth of 10 children of the 14th Earl of Strathmore and Kinghorne, who was descended from the Royal House of Scotland. Elizabeth was brought up in the family home at St Paul's Waldenbury in Hertfordshire, north of London. The family's Scottish home was at Glamis Castle and it was here that they occasionally entertained the Royal Family.

Pocket fact 🚩

Elizabeth was brought up in a happy loving family and contin- ued this with her own daughters, reading books such as Peter Pan *and* Black Beauty *to them.*

Elizabeth was considered to be quite a catch in her younger days and was courted by many suitors. George VI pursued her relent- lessly after deciding he wanted to marry her. Elizabeth was reluc- tant as she was unsure that she wanted to be a member of the Royal Family, but she accepted his third proposal in January 1923. After the wedding Elizabeth took to official duties like a duck to water, enchanting everyone with her signature charm. This was to stand her in good stead once she became Queen and then during the Second World War when her ease with the public won them over completely and gave Elizabeth a special place in the heart of the nation.

Pocket fact 🚩

Elizabeth was notorious for her timekeeping. She was once very late for dinner and when she apologised to the King he replied, 'You are not late, my dear. I think we must have sat down early.'

When George VI died in 1952, Elizabeth was only 52 years old. She continued with her public duties, including over 40 visits abroad, and was patron to more than 350 charities. Elizabeth had a life-long love of Scotland and purchased Castle Mey in Scotland in 1953. She was an expert fly fisher, fishing for salmon and trout and owned a string of National Hunt (jump racing) horses. Elizabeth was very popular with the public and on her birthday she would come outside Clarence House in the Mall to acknowl- edge the good wishes of the assembled crowd. Elizabeth passed away in 2002 at the grand age of 101 years.

Royal remarks 🐕

On the death of his grandmother Prince Charles said, 'Her houses were always filled with an atmosphere of fun, laughter and affection, and I learnt so much from her of immense value to my life. She was quite simply the most magical grandmother you could possibly have, and I was utterly devoted to her.'

♛ HUSBAND: PRINCE PHILIP, ♛ THE DUKE OF EDINBURGH

(20 June 1921–)

Prince Philip was born in Corfu in 1921 as Prince Philip of Greece and Denmark. He was the only son of Prince Andrew of Greece, the younger brother of King Constantine of Greece. Philip's mother was Princess Alice of Battenberg, the sister of Earl Mountbatten. Due to political unrest in Greece in the early 1920s King Constantine was forced to abdicate and the family were evacuated by the Royal Navy.

Pocket fact 🎲

In 1923 the 18-month-old Philip was evacuated from Greece in an orange box.

In 1947 Philip renounced his title of prince when he became a naturalised British citizen and took the name 'Mountbatten', an anglicised version of his mother's surname Battenberg.

Philip began his schooling in France but then came to England and went to Cheam Preparatory School and eventually on to Gordonstoun in Scotland. Philip joined the Royal Navy at 18 and served in the Second World War. Philip married the Queen on 20 November 1947 (see p.14) and continued with his naval career until Elizabeth became Queen in 1952.

Pocket fact 🔖

Prince Philip was created the Duke of Edinburgh, Earl of Merioneth and Baron Greenwich with the style of His Royal Highness shortly before his marriage. In 1957 the Queen granted him the style and title of Prince of the United Kingdom and he is addressed as either 'Your Royal Highness' or 'Sir'.

When the young woman he fell in love with became Queen, everything changed for Philip. The Queen was prevented from including Philip in affairs of state; however, it is as a husband supporting the Queen and as a father that Philip's position is the strongest.

Philip has also taken on the role of the Queen's late father and manages the royal estates such as Windsor and Sandringham. Philip also has a love of horses and played polo until age caught up with him in 1971. He then took up carriage driving instead and represented Great Britain at several European and world four-in-hand driving championships.

Pocket fact 🔖

Philip is one of the few people to treat the Queen like an ordinary human being, once threatening to put her out of the car when she was tutting at his driving speed.

Philip is patron or president of over 800 organisations and has accompanied the Queen on all of her overseas and Commonwealth visits and tours around Britain. Philip's interests focus on scientific and technological research and development, the encouragement of sport, the welfare of young people, and conservation and the environment.

The Duke of Edinburgh Award

Known as the 'D of E', the Duke of Edinburgh Award began as a pilot award scheme set up by Philip in 1956. In the early 1950s Prince Philip was approached by Kurt Hahn, the founder of Gordonstoun (the school that Prince Philip had attended in the 1930s), about an award scheme. Hahn had already set up several schemes in Scotland to increase the physical fitness of young people and he now wanted to extend it nationwide so he approached Prince Philip, who was already involved with several youth initiatives. With Prince Philip's backing a committee was set up and the ethos of the Duke of Edinburgh Award of no competition and no membership while promoting compassion, skills, physical fitness and initiative was established.

The programme of activities can be done by anyone between the ages of 14 and 24 and there are three levels: bronze, silver and gold. The awards are given for volunteering, physical recreation, skills, expedition and for gold, a residential activity. The first gold awards were presented in 1958 and to date over four million people have taken part in more than 60 countries. For more details visit the D of E website (www.dofe.org).

♔ SISTER: PRINCESS MARGARET ♔

(21 August 1930–9 February 2002)

Princess Margaret Rose was the only sister of the Queen. Margaret was brought up without the burden of becoming Queen (unless something happened to Elizabeth), meaning she had a reputation as the family joker. She was fun-loving, and because of her father's own experiences as the younger sibling of a future monarch, George overindulged her.

Royal remarks 🐕

Marion Crawford, the Queen's and Margaret's governess, described Margaret as 'a plaything. She was warm and demonstrative, made to be cuddled and played with.'

In 1948 Margaret developed a very close relationship with her father's equerry (personal assistant to the King) Group Captain Peter Townsend, who at the time was married with two children, causing a great deal of concern in royal circles. In 1952 Peter Townsend's marriage ended, leaving the way clear for him and Margaret to be together. Following the coronation in 1953 the newspapers were full of the romance between Margaret and Peter.

Pocket fact 🎞

Margaret was seen to flick a piece of fluff off the jacket of Peter Townsend outside Westminster Abbey at the coronation. This intimate gesture sent the press into a frenzy of speculation.

The idea of a marriage of Peter Townsend, a divorced man, and Margaret was not popular with the government, and because he was divorced Margaret would have to renounce all her titles and become simply Mrs Peter Townsend. In October 1955 Margaret issued a statement to say that she would not be marrying Peter Townsend because 'Christian marriage is indissoluble'. A recently published letter has dispelled the notion that Margaret changed her mind about the marriage because of pressure from the Royal Family.

In 1958 Margaret met Anthony Armstrong-Jones, the photographer. They were married in May 1960 in Westminster Abbey. Anthony Armstrong-Jones was made the Earl of Snowdon and Viscount

Linley in October 1961. Margaret and Anthony had two children, David, born 3 November 1961, and Sarah, born 1 May 1964.

Margaret and Anthony were a very glamorous couple and moved in circles outside the norm for the Royal Family, socialising with people such as Rudolf Nureyev, Peter Sellers, Vidal Sassoon and Mary Quant. Unfortunately the marriage did not last and they divorced in 1978. In the 1990s, Margaret's health started to deteriorate and in 1993 and 2001 she suffered a series of strokes leading to her death in 2002.

Pocket fact 🚩

Princess Margaret's wedding in 1960 was the first royal wedding to be broadcast on television and over 20 million people tuned it to watch.

♛ SON: PRINCE CHARLES ♛

(14 November 1948–)

Married:

1. Lady Diana Spencer (29 July 1981; divorced 28 August 1996)

2. Camilla Parker Bowles (9 April 2005)

Children:

1. William (born 21 June 1982)

2. Harry (born 15 September 1985)

Line of succession: 1st

Prince Charles is the eldest son of the Queen and therefore the heir to the throne. Unlike previous generations of the Royal Family Charles was not educated at home but attended Hill House, a pre-preparatory school in West London from the age of eight. Charles was then a boarder at the same schools as his father,

Prince Philip, Cheam School in Berkshire, from 1957, and then Gordonstoun in Scotland from 1962.

Pocket fact 🛈

When his grandfather died and his mother became Queen, Charles inherited the title of Duke of Cornwall and the Scottish titles of Duke of Rothesay, Earl of Carrick, Baron of Renfrew, Lord of the Isles and Prince and Great Steward of Scotland.

Gordonstoun was famous for its spartan regime of cold showers and early morning runs and Charles famously hated it. In 1966 Charles spent two terms at Timbertop, a remote annexe of Geelong Church of England Grammar School in Melbourne, Australia. Charles loved Timbertop where he could forget about being Prince Charles. He passed five GCE 'O' levels and two GCE 'A' levels (equivalent to GCSE today) and went to university at Trinity College, Cambridge in 1967. He studied archaeology, and physical and social anthropology in his first year and then history for the next two years with a break to study for one term at University College of Wales in Aberystwyth, where he studied Welsh and the history of the principality. Charles was the first heir to the throne to take a degree and was awarded a 2.ii in 1970.

Pocket fact 🛈

On 1 July 1970 Charles was invested by the Queen at Caernarfon Castle as the Prince of Wales. The title is traditionally granted to the heir apparent of the reigning monarch.

In keeping with the tradition of the Royal Family, Charles joined the RAF in 1971. Charles had already obtained his private pilot licence and went on to qualify as a jet pilot. In September 1971 Charles joined the Royal Navy College at Dartmouth, the same college his father had attended. In 1974 Charles was given the command of his own ship, the minesweeper HMS *Bronnington*, for the last 10 months of his active service with the Royal Navy, which ended in December 1976. In 1978 Charles was appointed Colonel-in-Chief of the Parachute Regiment and took part in a parachute training course.

Pocket fact 🗒

Charles was a keen polo player, playing his first match in 1963 when he was 15. He continued to play until 2005, playing his final match at the age of 57.

Charles undertakes numerous overseas visits on behalf of the monarchy and is patron of more than 400 organisations. Charles's most notable and successful charity is the 'Prince's Charities' (which incorporates the Prince's Trust), a not-for-profit organisa-tion that raises over £120m annually for a variety of causes including enterprise, health, the built environment, responsible business and the natural environment and is the largest multi-cause charitable enterprise in the UK.

Pocket fact 🗒

Charles is a committed environmentalist, and has installed solar panels, woodchip boilers and rainwater collection at Highgrove House.

Charles's food company, Duchy Originals, produces over 200 organic products, in partnership with the supermarket Waitrose, including biscuits, jam and meat, and was established in 1990. The profits from the sale of the products all go towards the Prince's Charities.

Pocket fact 🎟

The Prince's Trust holds an annual concert in Hyde Park. The musicians all give their time for free and in 2011 over 100,000 people attended the concert with all the proceeds going to the Trust, which helps over 50,000 young people a year.

♛ DAUGHTER: PRINCESS ANNE ♛

(15 August 1950–)

Married:

1. Captain Mark Phillips (14 November 1973; divorced April 1992)

2. Vice Admiral Timothy Laurence (12 December 1992)

Children:

1. Peter Phillips (born 15 November 1977)

2. Zara Phillips (born 15 May 1981)

Grandchildren:

1. Savannah Phillips (born 29 December 2010)

Line of succession: 10th

Princess Anne is the second child and only daughter of the Queen. Anne's official title of Princess Royal (only ever held by the eldest daughter of the monarch) was awarded by the Queen in 1987. Anne started her education at home and moved to the boarding school Beneden in Kent in 1963 when she was 13 years old. Anne left school with six GCE 'O' levels and two GCE 'A' levels.

Pocket fact 🔖

At the age of eight Anne realised that the guards on duty had to 'present arms' to members of the Royal Family when they passed, so she used to walk backwards and forwards until the Queen spotted her and called her in and gave her a royal telling off!

Anne was brought up with horses and first sat on a horse when she was two years old. In 1968 Anne was given her first horse and came seventh in the Novice Class of the Windsor Horse Trials. This was the beginning of a long and distinguished career in the world of three-day eventing (dressage, cross country and show jumping). Anne's equestrian wins included in 1971 individual European Three-Day Event at Burghley, individual and team silver at the European Three-Day Event Championship. Anne also competed in the 1976 Montreal Olympics as a member of the British three-day event team.

Pocket fact 🔖

Anne is well known for being fearless not only in her riding but also for firing a gun from a Chieftain tank when on a visit to the 14/20 Hussars.

Anne's fearlessness stood her in good stead when on 20 March 1974 a kidnap attempt was made on her and her husband Mark Phillips. On their way to Buckingham Palace a car blocked their route and Ian Ball got out and fired six shots. Anne's royal protection officer managed to fire at the man before he was wounded and two of the bullets also struck Ann's chauffeur and a passer-by. Ian Ball then climbed in the Rolls Royce and told Anne he intended to hold her to ransom for £2m or £3m and to get out of the car with him. She told him 'not bloody likely' and got out of the car on the other side. Eventually Ian Ball was arrested by a policeman who had heard the shots.

Anne began public engagements alone when she was just 18 and is reputedly the hardest working member of the Royal Family, undertaking over 500 engagements in 2008. Anne has been President of Save the Children Fund since 1970 and has travelled to countries such as Indonesia, China, Cambodia, Vietnam, Ethiopia and Malawi on behalf of the organisation. Anne is also the British Representative of the International Olympic Association and was part of the successful London bid for the 2012 Olympics.

Pocket fact 🎱

In 1987 Anne appeared on the long-running BBC television sports panel game A Question of Sport, *where the team captain, the footballer Emlyn Hughes, mistook a picture of her for a male jockey.*

♔ SON: PRINCE ANDREW ♔

(19 February 1960–)

Married: Sarah Ferguson (19 March 1986; divorced May 1996)

Children:

1. Princess Beatrice (born 8 August 1988)

2. Princess Eugenie (born 23 March 1990)

Line of succession: 4th

Prince Andrew is the third child and second son of the Queen. Andrew was educated at home until he went to Heatherdown Preparatory School, Ascot at the age of eight where he remained until he was 13. Andrew then followed his father and older brother to Gordonstoun in Scotland.

Pocket fact 🔟

Prince Andrew was created the Duke of York by the Queen on his marriage to Sarah Ferguson. The title is traditionally given to the second son of the monarch.

Andrew left school in 1979 and joined the Royal Navy. His career lasted 20 years and included undertaking the Royal Marine training course, learning to fly Sea King helicopters and commanding the Hunt class minehunter HMS *Cottesmore*. On leaving active service he became a staff officer at the Ministry of Defence responsible for Frigate and Destroyer aviation. When Andrew left the Royal Navy, he became the UK's Special Representative for International Trade and Investment, a role which he gave up in 2011. Andrew is patron to over 100 organisations including 'Fight for Sight', 'Defeating Deafness' and the British Deaf Association.

Pocket fact 🔟

Prince Andrew saw active service in 1982 during the Falklands War including flying anti-submarine warfare and casualty evacuation, transport and search and air rescue.

👑 SON: PRINCE EDWARD 👑

(10 March 1964–)

Married: Sophie Rhys-Jones (19 June 1999)

Children:

1. Lady Louise (born 8 November 2003)

2. James, Viscount Severn (born 17 December 2007)

Line of succession: 7th

Prince Edward is the third son and fourth child of the Queen. Edward was educated at home until he was seven and then he went to Gibbs School, a pre-preparatory school, in Kensington. Edward then went to the same schools as his brother Andrew, Heatherdown Preparatory School, Ascot and Gordonstoun. Andrew passed GCE A levels in history, English literature, and economic and political studies, and went on to study at Jesus College, Cambridge, graduating with a bachelor of arts in 1986.

Pocket fact 🖍

Whilst at Gordonstoun, Edward achieved gold award in the Duke of Edinburgh's award scheme set up by his father Prince Philip.

Whilst Edward was at school and university he developed an interest in drama and appeared in a number of productions. After university Edward spent a short time in the Royal Marines and then went on to pursue his love of drama, working for Andrew Lloyd Webber's Really Useful Company. As a production assistant he worked on productions such as *Cats*, *The Phantom of the Opera* and *Starlight Express*, where he was known as Edward Windsor.

In 2002 Edward withdrew from Ardent Productions, the production company he set up, to take on some of the Queen's workload and support her in her golden jubilee year. He is patron of a number of charities and organisations and is a trustee of the Duke of Edinburgh's Award in the UK, trustee of the International Award Foundation, and chairman of the International Council of the International Award Association (which operates in 126 countries around the world).

Pocket fact 🖍

Edward dated the musical theatre star Ruthie Henshall for three years after they met working on the West End show Cats.

♚ GRANDSON: PETER PHILLIPS ♚

(15 November 1977–)

Parents: Princess Anne and Captain Mark Phillips

Married: Autumn Kelly (17 May 2008)

Children: Savannah Phillips (born 29 December 2010)

Line of succession: 11th

Peter Phillips was born at St Mary's Hospital, Paddington, London and was christened Peter Mark Andrew Phillips on 22 December 1977 in the Music Room of Buckingham Palace. Peter went to Port Regis Preparatory School, Shaftesbury, Dorset, and then on to Gordonstoun and Exeter University where he graduated with a degree in sports science in 2000. Peter Phillips currently works for the Royal Bank of Scotland and does not carry out any royal duties.

Pocket fact 🚩

Peter and Zara Phillips do not have royal titles as titles can only be passed down from the father. So if you are a prince, your daughter is automatically a princess, but a princess's children do not automatically receive titles. The Queen could have given them titles but Princess Anne refused titles for her children because she wanted them to have ordinary lives out of the limelight.

♚ GRANDDAUGHTER: ♚ ZARA PHILLIPS

(15 May 1981–)

Parents: Princess Royal, Princess Anne, and Captain Mark Phillips

Married: Mike Tindall (30 July 2011)

Line of succession: 14th

Zara Phillips was born at St Mary's Hospital, Paddington and christened Zara Anne Elizabeth on 27 July 1981 at St George's Chapel, Windsor. Zara was educated at Port Regis Preparatory School, Shaftesbury, Dorset, and then Gordonstoun and Exeter University, where she qualified as a physiotherapist specialising in equine physiotherapy.

Pocket fact 🎯

Zara Phillips met her husband Mark Tindall, the England international rugby player, at the 2003 Rugby World Cup in Australia.

Zara participated in many sports such as hockey, athletics and gymnastics at school but with two parents who excelled in equestrian sport it was not surprising that in 2005 she won the European Eventing Championship individual and team gold medals on her horse Toytown at Blenheim, Oxfordshire. In 2006 in Aachen, Germany, Zara won the individual gold and team silver in the Eventing World Championship, also on Toytown. Zara Phillips is only the third rider to have achieved both titles.

Pocket fact 🎯

Zara Phillips was awarded an MBE (Member of the British Empire) for her services to equestrianism in 2007. Zara was the first senior royal to achieve this award. In 2006 Zara was voted the BBC Sports Personality of the Year by the public, 35 years after her mother had achieved the same award.

Zara was unable to compete at the 2008 Olympics due to an injury to her horse but she is currently hoping to be part of the British team at the London Olympics in 2012. Zara is involved with a number of charities including Inspire, for those with spinal cord injuries, Sargent Cancer Care for Children, and is patron of the Mark Davies Injured Riders Trust.

♔ GRANDSON: PRINCE WILLIAM ♔

(21 June 1982–)

Parents: Prince Charles, Prince of Wales, and Diana, Princess of Wales

Married: Catherine Middleton (29 April 2011)

Line of succession: 2nd

Prince William is the eldest son of Prince Charles and Diana, Princess of Wales. He is the Queen's third grandchild and heir to the throne after his father. William was born on 21 June 1982 at St Mary's Hospital, Paddington, London at 9.03pm and weighed 7lbs 1½ oz. William was christened William Arthur Philip Louis at Buckingham Palace in the Music Room by Dr Robert Runcie, the Archbishop of Canterbury.

Pocket fact 🔧

Prince William was the first heir to the throne to be born in a hospital.

William was educated at Mrs Mynors Nursery School, Notting Hill, and at Wetherby School, also in Notting Hill. William attended Ludgrave Preparatory School in September 1990 but both his parents were reluctant for William to be a full-time boarder so he came home at weekends. William then went on to Eton College, Berkshire, at the age of 13 and achieved A levels in geography, biology and history of art.

Pocket fact 🔳

Unlike his father Prince Charles, who was sent away to school, William was never far from the Royal Family as Eton College is just across the River Thames from Windsor Castle.

Prince William was 15 years old when his mother Princess Diana died in a car crash in Paris on 31 August 1997. One of the most moving images was that of the two young princes walking with Charles and Prince Philip behind the coffin of their mother.

Instead of going straight on to university, William took a 'gap year' and worked as a volunteer with Raleigh International in Chile, where he helped build walkways, taught English and prepared for survival exercise with the Horse Guards in Belize, the regiment he was to join later. William also worked on a British dairy farm where he was up early milking the cows and cleaning out the cowsheds.

William went to the University of St Andrews in Fife, Scotland, to study History of Art but later changed to Geography gaining a 2.i when he graduated in 2005. Whilst preparing for the Regular Commissions Board for entry into the Royal Military Academy Sandhurst, William embarked on a period of work experience, including working at a number of financial institutions in the City of London and on a country estate to learn about land management. He also joined an RAF mountain rescue team in Wales.

Pocket fact 🔳

It was at St Andrews that William met his future wife, Catherine Middleton.

William joined the Royal Military Academy at Sandhurst as an officer cadet and was commissioned as an officer in front of the Queen in December 2006. William joined the Household Cavalry Regiment, whose operational role is in armoured vehicles (The

Blues and Royals), as second lieutenant. William went on to train as a search and rescue pilot with the RAF, graduating in 2010.

William proposed to his long-time girlfriend Catherine Middleton on holiday in Kenya in October 2010 and they were married in Westminster Abbey on 29 April 2011. On his marriage to Catherine, William was given the title Duke of Cambridge by the Queen.

Royal remarks

William proposed to Catherine with his mother's engagement ring and later said: 'As you may have recognised, it's my mother's engagement ring so of course it is very special to me and Kate's very special to me now as well, and it's only right the two are put together.'

Despite his work as a search and rescue pilot, William still continues with the example set by his grandmother and father and undertakes official royal engagements. In 2009 William and Harry founded their own charity 'The Foundation of Prince William and Prince Harry', which focuses on helping young people who are disadvantaged or in need of guidance; the environment, especially to find better and more sustainable ways of living; and the armed forces, supporting servicemen and women who have served their country.

William is the patron of 19 charities and organisations including Centrepoint, the charity for the homeless, and Tusk Trust, which finds a way for a peaceful co-existence between Africa's people and its wildlife. He is President of the Royal Marsden Hospital, Patron of Mountain Rescue England and Wales and the English Schools' Swimming Association. In January 2010, as a tribute to his grandmother, the Queen, William became Patron of The Queen Elizabeth II Fields. The trust plans to protect and create hundreds of playing fields in honour of the Queen's Diamond Jubilee in 2012.

Pocket fact

William has continued with his grandmother's love of horses and horse riding. He is a skilful polo player like his grandfather Philip and father Charles. William is also a keen skier and enjoys watching both football and rugby and riding his powerful Italian motorbike.

♔ GRANDSON: PRINCE HARRY ♔

(15 September 1984–)

Parents: Prince Charles, Prince of Wales, and Diana, Princess of Wales

Line of succession: 3rd

Harry is the second son of Prince Charles and was born at St Mary's Hospital, Paddington, London, on 15 September 1984. He was christened Henry Charles Albert David by the Archbishop of Canterbury at St George's Chapel at Windsor Castle. Harry attended the same schools as William, and went to Eton College in 1998.

Pocket fact

Although christened Henry, Prince Charles and Princess Diana decided that he would be known as 'Harry', which is a nickname for Henry. The most famous Harry was Henry VIII, who was also known as 'Great Harry'.

Harry gained two A levels in art and geography, and he spent his gap year in Australia. He spent two months as a jackeroo (worker on a cattle ranch) in Tooloombilla, Queensland. Harry then worked for several charities in Lesotho, Southern Africa, including an Aids orphanage, where he made a television documentary called *The Forgotten Kingdom: Prince Harry in Lesotho* to highlight the plight of children and adults with Aids. Together with Prince Seeiso of the Lesotho Royal Family, Harry founded the 'Sentebale' (which means 'forget me not') charity, which helps orphans and disadvantaged children of Lesotho.

Harry passed his Regular Commissions Board for entry into the Royal Military Academy Sandhurst in 2005, and when he started his army cadet training course he was known as 'Officer Cadet Wales'. Harry completed his training in April 2006 and joined the Household Cavalry (Blues and Royals) armoured division. In 2008 Harry served 10 weeks in Afghanistan with his regiment but had to return home early after reports of his whereabouts appeared on a US website.

Pocket fact

Harry's job was JTAC (joint tactical air coordination) which meant he was responsible for calling in air cover for troops on the ground.

In January 2008 Harry began his training with the Army Air Corps to become a pilot and in March 2011 he qualified to fly Apache helicopters. In April 2008 Harry was promoted to the rank of lieutenant and from spring 2012 he is eligible to return to frontline fighting. Harry is patron to only a few organisations due to his military commitments, which include 'The Foundation of Prince William and Prince Harry', Walking with the Wounded, the Young Army Benevolent Fund Project, the Rugby Football Union, and the Rugby Football Injured Players Foundation.

Pocket fact

In 2004 Harry trained as a rugby development officer and visited schools encouraging young people to take up the sport.

♔ GRANDDAUGHTER: PRINCESS ♔ BEATRICE OF YORK

(8 August 1988–)

Parents: Prince Andrew, Duke of York, and Sarah, Duchess of York

Line of succession: 5th

Beatrice was born at Portland Hospital, London, and christened Beatrice Elizabeth Mary in the Chapel Royal in St James's Palace. Beatrice attended Upton House School, Windsor, and then Coworth Park School in 1995. At St George's School in Ascot she gained three A levels and was elected head girl. Beatrice graduated from Goldsmiths University of London in 2007 with a 2.i in history and history of ideas. Beatrice is involved with a number of charities and in 2010 was the first member of the Royal Family to run the London Marathon in aid of Children in Crisis.

Pocket fact 🛈

Beatrice wore a hat designed by Philip Treacy at the wedding of Prince William and Catherine that became the subject of much press and public comment. The 'offending' hat was auctioned for charity on eBay, and raised £81,000, which was donated to UNICEF and Children in Crisis.

♔ GRANDDAUGHTER: PRINCESS ♔ EUGENIE OF YORK

(23 March 1990–)

Parents: Prince Andrew, Duke of York, and Sarah, Duchess of York

Line of succession: 6th

Eugenie was born at Portland Hospital, London, and christened Eugenie Victoria Helena at St Mary Magdalene Church, Sandringham. Eugenie attended Winkfield Montessori from 1992 to 1993 and then attended the same schools as her sister Beatrice. She then boarded at Marlborough College, Wiltshire, gaining three A levels and went on to Newcastle University to study a 2.i combined honours degree in art history, English literature and politics. Eugenie's official duties were limited at that time as she was concentrating on her studies.

Pocket fact 🚩

Eugenie was the first royal baby to have a public christening.

♔ GRANDDAUGHTER: ♔ LADY LOUISE

(8 November 2003–)

Parents: Prince Edward, Earl of Wessex, and Sophie, Countess of Wessex

Line of succession: 9th

Louise was born at Frimley Park Hospital, Surrey and christened Louise Alice Elizabeth Mary on 24 April 2004 at the private chapel at Windsor Castle.

Pocket fact 🚩

Lady Louise was one of the bridesmaids at the wedding of Prince William and Catherine Middleton in 2011.

♔ GRANDSON: JAMES, ♔ VISCOUNT SEVERN

(17 December 2007–)

Parents: Prince Edward, Earl of Wessex, and Sophie, Countess of Wessex

Line of succession: 8th

James was born at Frimley Park Hospital and christened James Alexander Philip Theo at the private chapel at Windsor Castle.

♔ GREAT-GRANDDAUGHTER: ♔ SAVANNAH PHILLIPS

(29 December 2010–)

Parents: Peter Phillips and Autumn Phillips

Line of succession: 12th

Savannah Phillips was born at Gatcombe Park, the home of Princess Anne, on 29 December 2010.

♔ THE HOUSE OF WINDSOR ♔

The House of Windsor is the surname and house/dynasty name of the Royal Family. Until the First World War, the Royal Family's surname was Saxe-Coburg Gotha after Prince Albert, the husband of Queen Victoria. In 1917 George V changed the name to Windsor after Windsor Castle because of the mounting anti-German feeling during the war.

Pocket fact 🎲

The very English and royal name of Windsor was the brainchild of the George V's private secretary Lord Stamfordham.

When the Queen married Prince Philip, the Prime Minister, Winston Churchill, and her private secretary, Alan Lascelles, advised the Queen not to change the royal surname from Windsor to Prince Philip's surname of Mountbatten, which would have given the children the surname Mountbatten-Windsor. However, in 1960 the Queen and the Duke of Edinburgh decided that in future whenever their children needed to use a surname it would be Mountbatten-Windsor, but the House name would remain Windsor.

♔ LINE OF SUCCESSION ♔

In the past the line of succession of the British monarchy relied on *primogeniture*, which meant that usually only male heirs accede to the throne. However, it can become complicated. The simple succession is if the current king or queen has two sons, as is in the case of Prince Charles, then the eldest son, Prince William inherits. If there is a daughter and son, regardless of their age the son would have taken precedence and inherited the throne. Only if there is no son would the monarch's daughters inherit the throne.

However, in 2011 the government announced that in future the first child would inherit the throne but this will only be brought in for any children born to Prince William, meaning the current line of succession still relies on *primogeniture*.

- Prince Andrew is the next eldest son of the Queen after Prince Charles. Andrew moved down the line of succession when Prince Charles had children. Andrew will move down again when Prince William or Prince Harry have children as they are above him in the line of succession.

- Although Princess Anne is the Queen's second child after Charles she moved down the line of succession when her younger brothers Andrew and Edward were born. Anne moved down again when Andrew and Edward had children.

- Prince Harry is currently third in the line of succession but he will move down when his elder brother Prince William has children.

The current line of succession

1. *Prince Charles, Prince of Wales*
2. *Prince William, Duke of Cambridge*
3. *Prince Henry (Harry) of Wales*
4. *Prince Andrew, Duke of York*
5. *Princess Beatrice of York*
6. *Princess Eugenie of York*
7. *Prince Edward, Earl of Wessex*
8. *James, Viscount Severn*
9. *Lady Louise Windsor*
10. *Princess Anne, Princess Royal*
11. *Peter Phillips*
12. *Savannah Phillips*
13. *Zara Phillips*

The Windsors

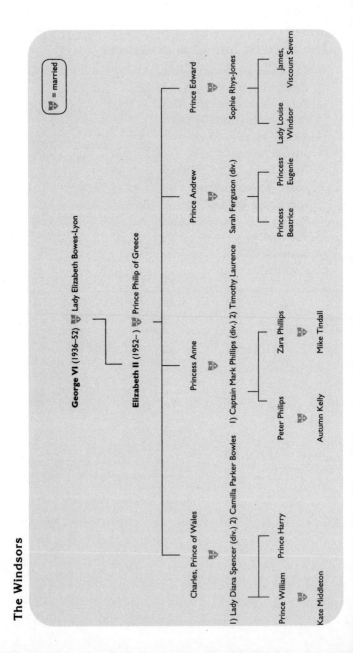

George VI (1936–52) 💍 Lady Elizabeth Bowes-Lyon

Elizabeth II (1952–) 💍 Prince Philip of Greece

Charles, Prince of Wales 💍
1) Lady Diana Spencer (div.) 2) Camilla Parker Bowles

Princess Anne 💍 1) Captain Mark Phillips (div.) 2) Timothy Laurence

Prince Andrew 💍 Sarah Ferguson (div.)

Prince Edward 💍 Sophie Rhys-Jones

Prince William 💍
Kate Middleton

Prince Harry

Peter Philips 💍
Autumn Kelly

Zara Phillips 💍
Mike Tindall

Princess Beatrice

Princess Eugenie

Lady Louise Windsor

James, Viscount Severn

💍 = married

3

THE QUEEN'S ROLE AND POWERS

The Queen is a part of our lives, we see her face every time we spend money or lick a stamp but what exactly is her role and what powers does she have? This chapter will explain the powers of the Queen today and what her roles as Head of the Nation, Head of State and Head of the Commonwealth of Nations entail.

♛ THE QUEEN'S TITLES ♛

The Queen's full title is:

> 'Queen Elizabeth the Second, by the Grace of God Queen of this Realm and of Her other Realms and Territories, Head of the Commonwealth, Defender of the Faith.'

The Queen also holds the titles of Duke of Lancaster, the Duke of Normandy and Lord of Mann. The Queen is Head of State of the United Kingdom, which consists of England, Wales, Scotland and Northern Ireland. This may sound rather grand but what do these titles actually mean in terms of the Queen's duties and powers?

Pocket tip ●

On first meeting the Queen you address her as 'Your Majesty' and thereafter as 'Ma'am' (as in jam).

QUEEN OF THIS REALM AND OF HER OTHER REALMS AND TERRITORIES

The title 'Queen of this Realm' refers to Elizabeth being Queen of England and Wales, Scotland and Northern Ireland. The Queen's other realms and territories are 15 of the countries which used to belong to the British Empire and now belong to the Commonwealth.

The Commonwealth

The British Commonwealth was founded in 1931 and in 1947 it changed its name to The Commonwealth. It has 54 member states, all of which were part of the British Empire. It is a voluntary association of independent states in the business of promoting democracy, good government, human rights and economic development. The Queen is its head and is a 'symbol of their free association'.

Members of the Commonwealth

Antigua & Barbuda	Australia
(The) Bahamas	Bangladesh
Barbados	Belize
Botswana	Brunei Darussalam
Cameroon	Canada
Cyprus	Dominica
Fiji (suspended)	The Gambia
The Gambia	Ghana
Grenada	Guyana
India	Jamaica
Kenya	Kiribati
Lesotho	Malawi
Malaysia	Maldives
Malta Mauritius	Mozambique
Namibia	Nauru
New Zealand	Nigeria
Pakistan	Papua New Guinea

Rwanda	Samoa
Seychelles	Sierra Leone
Singapore	Solomon Islands
South Africa	Sri Lanka
St Kitts	St Lucia
St Vincent & the Grenadines	Swaziland
Tonga	Trinidad & Tobago
Tuvalu	Uganda
United Kingdom	United Republic of Tanzania
Vanuatu	Zambia

DEFENDER OF THE FAITH AND SUPREME GOVERNOR OF THE CHURCH OF ENGLAND

The Queen not only holds the title 'Defender of the Faith' but also 'The Supreme Governor of the Church of England'. The title 'Defender of the Faith' was awarded in 1521 to Henry VIII by Pope Leo X in recognition of his book *Defence of the Seven Sacraments*, which defended the sacrament of marriage and the supremacy of the Pope against the rise of Protestant Reformation. Monarchs continued to use this title despite the fact that in the 1530s Henry VIII broke with the Roman Catholic Church in Rome because it would not permit him to divorce his first wife Catherine of Aragon. Henry needed a divorce to marry Anne Boleyn and when it wasn't granted he decided to make himself 'Supreme Governor of the Church of England', a title that has been passed to every monarch since.

Pocket fact 🎞

If you look at the back of a British coin, around the Queen's head you will see the letters 'FD'; this stands for Fidei Defensor, *which is Latin for Defender of the Faith.*

The Queen's titles of 'Defender of the Faith and Supreme Governor of the Church of England' mean that the Queen is the

Head of the Church of England and the Church of Scotland as they are the recognised religions and as such it is the Queen's duty to defend them. The Queen's role as the Supreme Governor of the Church of England is to appoint archbishops and bishops in the Church of England (but not Scotland), on the advice of the prime minister from names selected by the Church Commission.

The archbishops, bishops and parish priests all swear an oath of allegiance to the Queen, and archbishops and bishops may not resign without her permission. The cathedrals and churches of the Church of England are under the direct control of the arch-bishops and bishops except if they are Royal Peculiars. These churches are under the direct control of the Queen, and depend-ing on the size of the church are either headed by a canon and deans or a chaplain.

The Royal Peculiars are:

- St George's Chapel, Windsor Castle
- the Chapel Royal, St James's Palace
- the Queen's Chapel, St James's Palace
- the Chapel Royal, Hampton Court
- the Chapel of St John the Evangelist in the Tower of London
- the Chapel of St Peter ad Vincula in the Tower of London
- the Royal Chapel of All Saints, Windsor
- the Queen's Chapel of the Savoy, London
- the Royal Foundation of St Katharine
- the Chapel of St Edward, King and Martyr, Cambridge
- the Palace of Holyroodhouse, Scotland
- the Collegiate Church of St Peter, Westminster (Westminster Abbey)
- the Chapel of St Mary Undercroft, the crypt of the former St Stephen's Chapel in the Palace of Westminster.

DUKE OF LANCASTER

As the reigning monarch, the Queen holds the title of the Duke of Lancaster and as head of the Duchy of Lancaster owns 18,200 hectares of land across England and Wales, including historic, rural and commercial properties. The income from the duchy is administered by the duchy chancellor and the duchy council is involved in a number of charities. The Duchy of Lancaster Benevolent Fund funds a variety of causes, primarily in the counties of Greater Manchester, Lancashire and Merseyside. These include the Everyman Theatre in Liverpool, Rochdale Cycling Club and the Merseyside Chinese Community Development Association.

Pocket fact 🎱

The Duchy of Lancaster owns the Savoy Estate in London (an area of land bounded by the Strand and Embankment made up of shops and offices, but not including the Savoy Hotel), the old Knaresborough Castle, Lancaster Castle and the tiny railway station of Goathland in Yorkshire, which was used in the Harry Potter *films as Hogsmeade Station, the stop for Hogwarts School.*

DUKE OF NORMANDY

The Queen's title of the Duke of Normandy comes from her role as head of the Channel Islands, a small group of islands off the coast of France. These islands are not part of the UK but are dependent territories of the Crown as they form part of the Queen's inheritance as the Duke of Normandy. When William the Conqueror, Duke of Normandy, successfully invaded England in 1066 and became William I, the Channel Islands were part of his lands and although the monarchy lost the rest of the lands of Normandy, it retained the Channel Islands. The Crown is responsible for the defence and international relations of the Channel Islands.

Pocket fact 🔖

The Channel Islands was the only part of the Queen's realm that was occupied by Germany during the Second World War.

LORD OF MANN

The Queen is Head of State of the Isle of Man, a small island located off the coast of northern England in the Irish Sea. The Isle of Man was under the control of Norway and in the 13th century under the Treaty of Perth was given to Scotland. In the 14th century it was acquired by England's King Edward I in a treaty with Scotland.

The island is a self-governing British Crown dependency and has its own representative government called the Tynwald. However, the Queen (who is known as the Lord of Mann on the island) is the ultimate authority acting through the Privy Council (see p.69). The Queen's representative on the island is the Lieutenant Governor, who is appointed by the Queen and has delegated power from the Queen to give Royal Assent (approval) to legislation dealing with local matters.

Pocket fact 🔖

In 2011 for the first time since the Royal Maundy Service (see p.102) began in the Middle Ages, 40 residents from the Isle of Man were given Maundy money by the Queen at the service held at Westminster Abbey.

♔ THE QUEEN'S ROLES ♔

As the monarch the Queen's role is to be Head of the Nation, Head of State, the Fount of Justice and Commander in Chief of the Armed Forces. The Queen also accredits British Ambassadors and receives diplomats from foreign states.

HEAD OF THE NATION

As Head of the Nation the Queen opens factories and museums, attends commemoration services and meets and greets as many people as possible. The Queen is also the focus of national identity, unity and pride as no matter what people's political views, religious beliefs or ethnicity, she represents the nation as a whole. The Queen also awards a variety of honours in recognition of those deserving people who have made a difference to their community and for merit and bravery.

Pocket fact 🛈

The Court Circular is published every day in The Times, The Telegraph *and* The Scotsman *newspapers. It details the official engagements carried out by the Queen and other members of the Royal Family. You can also see the royal engagements at the British Monarchy website (www.royal.gov.uk/LatestNewsand Diary/CourtCircular/Todaysevents.aspx).*

VISITS

The Queen has visited every part of the UK from the Shetland Isles to the Isles of Scilly. During the Queen's regional visits, she tries to meet as many ordinary people as she can. The Queen will be well briefed before each visit by her office on the people she will be visiting and any local issues that might be relevant.

Pocket fact 🛈

The Queen and her dressers always ensure that her dresses and hats are brightly coloured so she can be easily seen among the crowds.

The Queen's visits range from an umbrella factory in East London, The Royal Highland Show in Edinburgh, a Children's

Centre in Brighton, a chewing gum factory in Plymouth, the Chelsea Flower Show, or any organisation that she is patron of.

Throughout the year the Queen receives numerous requests from a variety of organisations. The Queen's private secretary (see p.120), in conjunction with the lord lieutenant based in each county, decides whether a visit should take place and what the Queen will visit. Sometimes if the Queen's office feels she has not visited an area of the country for a while, it will contact the relevant lord lieutenant to arrange a visit.

Pocket fact 🚩

The Queen was the first monarch to do the 'walkabout' (a walk where she meets and chats to the crowds) in 1970 to allow her to meet more people.

Lord Lieutenants

Lord Lieutenants are the Queen's representatives in each county of the UK. They are appointed by the Queen on the advice of the prime minister. The office of Lord Lieutenant was originally created in the 16th century by Henry VIII to control the local military forces of the crown. There are 98 lord lieutenants, and they escort members of the Royal Family on visits to their county and keep the Queen up to date with any local issues, particularly when a royal visit is planned.

Gifts for the Queen

The Queen has received a number of gifts on her regional visits including:

- *a London Underground sign that says 'Buckingham Palace'*
- *a model of the famous characters Wallace and Gromit and Morph*

- *a commemorative silver trowel after laying a foundation stone*
- *a silver model of a tunnelling machine used to tunnel the second Mersey Tunnel*
- *a book of hat designs created by local children from the Whitehawk Estate in Brighton.*

NATIONAL CELEBRATIONS

The nation looks to the Queen to reflect their emotions and to represent them, whether it be for those who died in the two world wars on the annual service of remembrance in November, the 300th anniversary of St Paul's Cathedral or the unveiling of a statue, such as that of the Queen Mother on the Mall in 2011.

When Diana died there was outrage that the flag on Buckingham Palace was not flown at half-mast as a mark of respect. But the Royal Standard (which is only flown if the Queen is in residence) is never flown at half-mast, not even for the death of a monarch. So the Queen agreed that even though she was in residence the flag could be changed to the Union flag (Union Jack) and that it would be flown at half-mast.

HEAD OF STATE

The Queen reigns but she does not govern. The Queen's role is to carry out constitutional and representational duties as Head of State. This is because the British monarchy is a constitutional monarchy, which means the right to make and pass legislation resides with the elected government in parliament and not the monarch.

The Queen's role as Head of State is not written down but has changed and developed and become accepted over the last 1,000 years since the reign of William the Conqueror. The Queen's con-stitutional duty provides the country with a stable and continuing head of state regardless of which political party is in power.

Pocket fact 🛈

The Queen and the Royal Family never vote or stand for election as they have to remain politically neutral. There is no law preventing them from doing so, but it is considered unconstitutional. They could vote or stand for election in the European Parliament though.

The Queen's representational duties are mainly official state visits which cement relationships between the UK and foreign nations and royal tours to the Commonwealth (see p.72).

The Queen and the government

The Queen's role in parliament is to grant royal assent (the Queen's agreement to make a bill a law) to all bills passed by parliament, on the advice of government ministers. The Queen's assent is automatic but she continues to have the right to be consulted, encourage or warn her ministers through regular meetings. The Queen also opens every new session of parliament (normally after the summer recess) and dissolves parliament when informed by the current prime minister of a forthcoming general election.

Pocket fact 🛈

After every general election, the leader of the winning political party drives from Downing Street to Buckingham Palace to be formally appointed by the Queen. The Queen then asks the potential prime minister if he or she can form a government (the answer will usually be 'yes'). This appears in the Court Circular (see p.63) as 'the prime minister kissed hands on appointment' as was originally done to demonstrate loyalty to the monarch.

Prime minister's weekly meeting

The Queen holds a weekly meeting with the prime minister on Wednesday evenings at Buckingham Palace, or by telephone, if either one of them is unavailable. The meeting lasts around an hour and takes place in the Queen's Audience Rooms. There is no written record of these meetings.

The meetings keep the Queen up to date with the legislative matters and international issues and give the prime minister the opportunity to speak to someone with a wealth of experience, an understanding of what it is to be prime minister and someone they can talk freely to, knowing that it would never be repeated or used in some way against them.

Royal remarks

'Only the corgis are present, if they had been bugged the Russians would have known all our secrets.'

John Major, British prime minister (1990–97).

The Queen has lived through the changing times of the past 60 years giving her an accumulated wealth of political experience. During her reign there has been the establishment of the European Economic Community (EEC) (the forerunner to the European Union), the Falklands and Gulf Wars, the granting of independence to British colonies, the fall of Communist Russia and of the Berlin Wall. The Queen has also met numerous heads of state, 11 US presidents (including President Truman and President Kennedy). She was the first monarch to address a joint session of the US Congress.

Pocket fact

Prime Minister David Cameron is the Queen's 13th prime minister, the first being Winston Churchill in 1952.

AUDIENCES

The Queen will also have a variety of official meetings or audiences with overseas ambassadors, senior members of the British and Commonwealth Armed Forces on their retirement and appointment, the Chief of the Defence Staff, the Poet Laureate, newly appointed bishops and judges and commanding officers of regiments prior to them taking up their appointment.

Pocket fact 🗲

Overseas ambassadors are required to present their letters of credence (the official accreditation from their country) to the Queen at Buckingham Palace on taking up their post.

RED BOXES

The Queen's famous red boxes are delivered to her every day by her private secretary, except on Christmas Day and Easter Sunday. They contain the account of the day in parliament, classified security briefings, embassy reports from around the world, information in the form of policy papers from her government ministers and Foreign and Commonwealth representatives, Cabinet documents, telegrams, letters and other state papers. They all have to be read and where necessary they have to be approved and signed. Often the Queen will work late into the night to complete the box so it can be returned the next day.

Vital statistics of the red boxes

- *When the Queen has to sign documents, whether official or unofficial her signature is* Elizabeth R. *The* R *stands for* Regina, *the Latin word for Queen.*
- *The boxes are lead-lined briefcases covered in red leather and stamped with the Queen's cypher of EIIR.*
- *The smaller box is a 'reading box' prepared by the Queen's private secretary containing up to 60 pieces of paper.*

- *The larger box is used at the weekends and has up to two days of reading.*
- *There are four keys to the box, one for the Queen and one for each of her three private secretaries.*
- *An incoming box has a white label that sticks out and reads 'The Queen'. When the boxes have been read the Queen turns the label around so it is returned to the correct private secretary.*
- *The design has not changed since the 1860s and they are also used by government ministers.*
- *The box is more often seen held by the Chancellor of the Exchequer on the day of the announcement of the government's budget.*

THE PRIVY COUNCIL

Originally the Privy Council was the name given to a group of ministers who were chief advisors to the monarch but as the power of parliament grew the council's role diminished. Today the role of the Privy Council is to oversee those organisations who have been awarded a royal charter. These charters are given to organisations that work in the public interest, such as the BBC or places of higher education. The Privy Council is also the court of final appeal for UK overseas territories and Crown dependencies and for those Commonwealth countries which have retained the right of appeal to the Queen, including Jamaica, Barbados, Antigua and Barbuda, Belize and Tuvalu. The Privy Council meets on average once a month at Buckingham Palace, Windsor and sometimes at Balmoral Castle.

Pocket fact 🛈

The meeting takes place in the 1844 room in Buckingham Palace so called because that is the year it was decorated for the visit of Emperor Nicholas I of Russia.

There are about 550 members of the Privy Council but only about four or five attend the meetings. The members include all cabinet members of the government, senior members of the Royal Family, senior judges, two archbishops, the speaker of the House of Commons, leaders of opposition parties, and leading Commonwealth spokesmen and judges.

At the meetings the Privy Council will obtain the Queen's formal approval to orders that have been approved by ministers, such as passing the power of ministers of the UK to the devolved assemblies of Scotland, Wales and Northern Ireland. The orders are issued 'by and with the advice of Her Majesty's Privy Council'. The Queen also approves proclamations (formal notices) through the Privy Council including the dissolution of parliament, coinage and the dates of certain bank holidays. The orders of the Privy Council are printed in the Court Circular (see p.63).

Pocket fact 🚩

The custom is for everyone to stand during the meetings, including the Queen. This dates from 1861 when Prince Albert died and the Privy Council stood during the meetings as a mark of respect. It has the advantage of making the meetings short!

REGIONAL PARLIAMENTS AND ASSEMBLIES

Today the Queen also has a role to play in regional parliaments and assemblies. In the Scottish Parliament the Queen grants royal assent to legislation and formally appoints the Scottish first minister, whom she meets regularly to keep her up to date. The Queen also receives a weekly report on the Scottish Parliament. In the Welsh Assembly the Queen formally appoints ministers and grants royal assent to its legislation. The Queen also holds meetings with the first minister of Wales but is usually kept up to date by her Westminster parliament ministers. In the Northern Ireland Assembly the Queen grants royal assent and is kept up to date by her Westminster parliament ministers.

Pocket fact 🛈

Under the 1772 Royal Marriages Act close members of the Royal Family need the consent of the Queen to marry. The act prevents the Royal Family from marrying anyone who is unsuitable. Prince William had to obtain the Queen's permission to marry Catherine Middleton. The notice of approval read 'consent is granted to our Most Dearly Beloved Grandson Prince William Arthur Philip Louis of Wales, K.G. and Our Trusty and Well-beloved Catherine Elizabeth Middleton'.

STATE VISITS

As Head of State it is part of the Queen's role to visit foreign countries on state visits and entertain other heads of state during their state visits to the UK. The Queen is also required to carry out official royal tours to the Commonwealth countries. These visits by arrangement with the government cement existing relationships and open up new relationships with emerging economies or recently independent countries such as China and Estonia. These visits can also be historically significant, such as the recent visit to the Republic of Ireland, where the Queen was the first British monarch to visit for over 100 years.

Pocket fact 🛈

The Queen has made over 256 official visits to over 132 countries. This includes over 76 state visits.

The state visit of the Queen is the catalyst for face-to-face discussions over matters of diplomacy, trade and culture that might otherwise not take place. When a visit has been suggested the head of state sends an official invitation to the Queen. The visit is then planned and the Queen and Duke of Edinburgh are consulted on the visit and itinerary. Once the preliminary plan of the visit is complete a reconnaissance visit takes place and the visit is finalised.

Pocket fact 🛈
Air traffic controllers keep an exclusion zone around the Queen's plane when it is flying to keep other planes at a safe distance. This is known as a 'purple carpet'.

Despite being in her eighties, the Queen still undertakes two to three state visits a year. The Queen's first visit after her coronation in 1955 was to Norway. The Queen has visited countries ranging from Chile, Latvia, Sudan and South Korea to the Vatican City to visit the Pope. The logistics of organising a trip like this is tremendous and range from who the Queen will meet, what visits she will undertake, the speeches, clothes and most important, security (see p.134).

Pocket fact 🛈
The Queen does not have a passport and uses RAF or chartered flights for overseas visits.

The Queen will be well briefed on the people she is going to meet and her itinerary by her private secretaries. The British embassy staff in the country being visited have a major role as they will be familiar with the locale and will help decide on the itinerary and normally host a banquet on behalf of the Queen. The visit often contains a mixture of formal and informal visits; for example when the Queen visited the USA in 2007 she had a day at the Kentucky Derby.

Royal tours to the Commonwealth

Royal tours are the same as state visits in that they cement and advance relationships with countries within the Commonwealth.

The Queen's visits are immensely popular and thousands of people will turn out to greet her. When the Queen visits the Commonwealth countries she often takes part in local ceremonies and customs that are somewhat out of the ordinary, for example:

- in Ceylon in 1954 there was a procession of 140 decorated elephants

- in Nigeria she witnessed the 'Great Charge' of 2,500 horse-men and 5,000 men on foot

- in Northern Sierra Leone half-naked girls danced a fertility dance

- in Fiji in 1954 the Queen drank the native *kava* drink from a coconut

- in 1985 in Belize she ate a gibnut, a small native rodent much like a rabbit.

Pocket fact 🗲

The Queen took over 100 dresses for her first royal tour in 1953. Many of the dresses incorporated national emblems in their embroidery of the countries she was visiting. In Australia the slim figure of the Queen was set off by a spectacular crino-line gown embroidered with sprays of wattle, the national flower of Australia.

Commonwealth Day

Every year on the second Monday in March the Queen attends Commonwealth Day celebrations in London. The celebrations include an inter-denominational service held in Westminster Abbey and a reception hosted by the Commonwealth Secretary-General at Marlborough House in London, the headquarters of the Commonwealth Secretariat. The Queen also broadcasts a speech to the Commonwealth nations on Commonwealth Day and her Christmas Day Broadcast is aired to the Commonwealth.

Pocket fact 🗝

Every four years one of the member countries hosts the Commonwealth Games and the Commonwealth Youth Games which are opened by the Queen. Glasgow will host the Commonwealth Games in 2014 and in 2015 Samoa will host the Commonwealth Youth Games.

VISITS BY A HEAD OF STATE

A state visit by a visiting head of state is of equal importance as the Queen making a state visit. As with outgoing state visits they give the government the chance to talk to other governments and the heads of state to get to know each other. The visit will normally be around two to three days where the head of state will stay at either Buckingham Palace or Windsor Castle.

The head of state will be presented formally to the Queen after which gifts will be exchanged before a formal luncheon. The impact of these grand occasions is immeasurable as it is the definitive gesture of friendship from the Queen and the British government to another nation. The highlight of the visit is the state banquet held in either the ballroom at Buckingham Palace or St George's Hall at Windsor Castle. Pre-dinner drinks are served in the Picture Gallery at Buckingham Palace and the Crimson and Green drawing rooms at Windsor Castle.

Pocket fact 🗝

The Queen's favourite drink is $1/3$ of gin and $2/3$ Dubonnet, with one slice of lemon and two ice cubes.

Top ten facts about state banquets

1. The Queen has given over 91 state banquets during her reign.
2. The table is laid with pieces from the George VI grand service of silver gilt (silver covered in gold), which includes 288 plates and enough cutlery for every course.
3. There are two pats of butter next to every plate and the Royal Cypher of EIIR is stamped on every pat.
4. Each place setting on the banqueting table is exactly 18 inches apart and one thumb length from the edge of the table.
5. The wine is selected from the 25,000 bottles in the wine cellar.
6. The Queen always inspects the laid table and flower arrangements.
7. Each person has six glasses — one each for red wine, white wine, water and port and two for champagne (one for dessert and one for toasts).
8. Music is played by one of the Guards Bands.
9. The waiting staff is directed by a discreetly placed set of traffic lights such as in the balcony in St George's Hall at Windsor Castle. Red means ready to serve and green means serve or clear.
10. If you eat slowly you don't eat, as plates are cleared when the Queen is finished!

The Queen has received over 1,600 gifts from state visits including:

- her favourite horse Burmese from Canada
- Lalique crystal sculpture of two horses from France
- jaguars and sloths from Brazil
- two black beavers from Canada

- two turtles from the Seychelles
- a Maori canoe from New Zealand
- an elephant called Jumbo from Cameroon
- a silver box containing a live baby crocodile from Gambia.

FOUNTAIN OF HONOURS

As Head of the Nation the Queen is the 'fountain of honours' as it is the Queen who confers the honours available, including life peerages, knighthoods and gallantry awards. The honours are awarded on the advice of the government's Cabinet Office and are given out twice a year in the New Year Honours List and the Queen's Birthday (official birthday) Honours list in June.

Pocket fact ❗

Since 1952, the Queen has conferred over 387,700 honours and awards.

There are two routes to being awarded an honour: nomination by a person or private or public organisation or a nomination from a private or public source sent to a government department. The nomination is then sent to the nominations team of the Honours and Appointments Secretariat and then it goes through a number of committees before the list is submitted to the prime minister and then the Queen for final approval. (See p.104 for more details on honours and investitures.)

Pocket fact ❗

The only honours that the Queen selects personally are the Order of the Garter, the Order of the Thistle, the Order of Merit, the Royal Victorian Order and the Royal Victorian Chain, Royal Medals of Honour and Medals for Long Service.

HEAD OF THE ARMED FORCES

The Queen is Head of the Armed Forces of the UK, namely the Royal Navy, Royal Marines, Royal Air Force and the Army. The Queen is the Commander-in-Chief of the British Armed Forces and the armed forces swear allegiance to the Queen.

The history of the monarch as the head of the armed forces dates back to when the reigning monarch was not only the ruler but the best military commander. British history is littered with monarchs who lost their crown to more successful military commanders, such as William the Conqueror who defeated Harold at the Battle of Hastings in 1066 or Richard III who lost his crown to Henry VII at the Battle of Bosworth in 1485. Over time it has become less necessary for the monarch to be a military commander as the armed forces became more professional, but the tradition of the monarch as the head of the armed forces has remained.

Pocket fact 🔑

As Head of State the queen has the power to declare war and peace which dates from the time when the monarch was responsible for equipping, raising and maintaining the navy and army. Today this would be carried out on the advice of the government.

Today, under British constitutional law the armed forces are subordinate to the monarch but it is parliament that maintains them during peace time and the prime minister and government have the actual power over the armed forces.

Colonel-in-Chief

The Queen is Colonel-in-Chief to over 15 army regiments including all five Guards regiments – the Welsh, Irish, Scots, Coldstream and Grenadier (for more details on the Guards regiments see p.88) – and the Household Cavalry (see p.89 for more details). The Queen is also Colonel-in-Chief to a number of regiments of Commonwealth countries including the King's Own Calgary Regiment (Canada), the Royal Australian Engineers and the Royal New Zealand Infantry Regiment. The Queen is Air Commodore-in-Chief of the Royal Auxiliary Air Force and the Royal Air Force Regiment.

As Colonel-in-Chief or Air Commodore-in-Chief the Queen is a patron and has no involvement in operational duties. As patron the Queen will present awards to the members of the armed forces, visit their headquarters and speak with the families. The Queen's role is to maintain the connection between the armed services and the monarchy.

The Elizabeth Cross

In 2009, in a broadcast on the British Forces Broadcasting Service, the Queen announced that an award, which she had asked to bear her name, was to be given to the recognised next of kin of those who were killed in frontline or terrorist attacks. The award is called the Elizabeth Cross and is accompanied by a memorial scroll signed by the Queen. The cross is made of silver with a laurel wreath passing between the arms which bear a rose (representing England), a thistle (representing Scotland), a daffodil (representing Wales) and a shamrock (representing Ireland). The centre of the cross has the Queen's cypher EIIR. It is accompanied by a smaller lapel badge version. In 2010 the cross was awarded to the families of 10 Norfolk servicemen and women who had lost their lives in conflict.

The Queen and the Royal Family have always had a very strong link with the armed services as her father George VI served in the Royal Navy and fought in the First World War. Prince Philip served in the Royal Navy during the Second World War and the Queen's sons Charles, Andrew and Edward have all served in the armed services. The Queen's grandsons William and Harry have continued the military tradition. William completed officer training at Sandhurst and joined the Household Cavalry and is currently in the Royal Air Force serving as a search and rescue pilot. Harry also completed officer training at Sandhurst and served in the Household Cavalry and for two months in Afghanistan. Harry is currently on secondment to the Army Air Corps where he is training to be an Apache attack helicopter pilot.

THE ROYAL STANDARD AND ROYAL COAT OF ARMS

The Royal Standard is the Queen's flag which flies above her palaces when she is in residence, on her car and aircraft (when on the ground). The flag is divided into four sections:

- the top left and bottom right has yellow lions lying down on a red background (representing England)

- the top right has a red lion standing and looking right on a yellow background (representing Scotland)

- the bottom left has a yellow harp on a blue background (representing Ireland).

The Royal Coat of Arms is used in the administration and government of the country appearing on official documents, coins, churches and public buildings and on the products and goods of royal warrant holders (companies and suppliers who have supplied goods to the Queen).

The Coat of Arms is a shield with the pattern of the Royal Standard supported by a yellow standing English lion on the left wearing a crown and a white Scottish unicorn on the right. The shield is surrounded by a blue garter with the motto *Honi soit qui mal y pense* ('Evil to him who evil thinks'), which represents the Order of the Garter (see p.95). Underneath is the motto of the Sovereign, *Dieu et mon droit* ('God and my right').

4

ROYAL EVENTS AND CEREMONIES

The Queen has attended many public and historic events through-out her reign, from religious ceremonies to jubilee celebrations and national events to sombre memorials. This chapter will describe a range of events from her once-in-a-lifetime event, her coronation in 1953, as well as ceremonies that occur throughout the year such as the Garter Service at Windsor Castle, the Remembrance Service, the State Opening of Parliament and Royal Ascot.

Pocket tip ●

To find out what royal events are taking place and where, go to the 'ceremonies and events' map on the British monarchy website (www.royal.gov.uk/RoyalEventsandCeremonies/Ceremoniesandev entsmap/Gallery.aspx).

♛ ONCE IN A LIFETIME: ♛ THE CORONATION

The Queen's coronation took place on 2 June 1953 at Westminster Abbey, following her accession to the throne on 6 February 1952 on the death of her father King George VI. The coronation day began with the 27-year-old Queen and her hus-band Prince Philip leaving Buckingham Palace for Westminster Abbey in the Gold State Coach built for George III in 1762. The coach was pulled by eight grey horses called Cunningham, Tovey, Noah, Tedder, Eisenhower, Snow White, Tipperary and McCreery.

Pocket fact 🛈

Since the coronation of William the Conqueror in 1066, nearly every coronation has taken place in Westminster Abbey (with the exception of Edward V and Edward VIII). Queen Elizabeth II was the 39th monarch to be crowned at Westminster Abbey.

The sight of the coronation procession was magnificent with the red tunics and bearskin hats of the Guard's regiments lining the streets and the blue and red coats and shining helmets of the Household Cavalry following the Gold State Coach. This was a reason to cheer and celebrate; the crowd was so deep that people used cardboard periscopes so they could see over the heads of the people in front.

Preparations for the day

- *Westminster Abbey was closed for six months while the seating for 8,251 guests was installed.*
- *In Glasgow 31 blue and gold carpets were made for the nave and aisle of Westminster Abbey totalling 2,964 yards.*
- *In Bradford 4,000 yards of velvet were woven to cover the 2,000 chairs and 5,700 stools for the guests.*
- *In Braintree, Essex, it took 10 weeks to hand-weave the 20 yards of purple velvet for the Queen's coronation robe.*
- *12 seamstresses took 3,500 hours to embroider the EIIR and a border of wheat ears and olive branches in gold on the coronation robe.*
- *The silk for the embroidery on the purple Robe of State came from a silk farm in Lullingstone, Kent, the same farm that had made the material for the Queen's wedding dress.*
- *1,500 yards of silk was woven for hangings to decorate Westminster Abbey.*
- *The Queen's robe of crimson velvet was edged with ermine and two rows of hand-made embroidered gold lace and gold filigree work. It measured 21 feet from her shoulder.*

THE CORONATION CEREMONY

The coronation service descends directly from the service used for King Edgar at Bath in AD973 and is full of religious elements, historic meaning and pageantry. On the day, Westminster Abbey was full to the roof with people in every available space possible. Additional seating was even built in the archways and in the transept; 129 nations and territories were represented at the service.

The dress the Queen wore was designed by Norman Hartnell and was embroidered with floral emblems, representing some of the different nations of which she is head:

- Australia: wattle
- Canada: maple leaf
- Ceylon: lotus
- England: rose
- Ireland: shamrock
- New Zealand: fern
- Pakistan: wheat and jute
- Scotland: thistle
- South Africa: protea
- Wales: leek.

Pocket fact 🛈

The coronation chair or King Edward's chair has been used for the coronation of every monarch since 1308, except for William III and Mary II who were crowned in 1689 as joint monarchs in replica chairs, and Edward V in 1483 and Edward VIII in 1936 who were not crowned.

The Queen wore the George IV State Diadem (see p.158) and walked up the aisle to the central space of the abbey which had been covered in gold carpet and is described as the 'coronation theatre'. There was a raised dais with the throne and behind it, nearer the altar, the King Edward chair or coronation chair, where the actual coronation took place.

The Queen attended several rehearsals in Westminster Abbey and at Buckingham Palace where the ballroom was marked out to replicate the abbey so she could practise walking with sheets pinned to her shoulders. The Queen also had to practise walking in the coronation robes as they are so heavy. The super-tunica weighs 23lbs and the St Edward's Crown (see p.156) weighs 4lb 12 ounces and is made of solid gold.

The Coronation took place in six parts and was officiated by the Archbishop of Canterbury, Dr Geoffrey Fisher.

The Recognition

The Archbishop presented the Queen to the congregation and they shouted 'God Save the Queen'.

The coronation robes

- *The newly made* colobium sindonis *(Latin for 'shroud tunic' – a loose linen garment)*
- *The gold supertunica (a full-length sleeved coat made of gold cloth)*
- *The mantle (a long gold cloak embroidered with eagles, crowns and fleurs-de-lis and roses, thistles and shamrocks)*
- *The stole (a scarf embroidered with the crosses of national saints of George for England, Andrew for Scotland and Patrick for Ireland and symbolic plants).*

The coronation oath

The Queen swore to govern faithfully with justice and mercy, to uphold the gospel and to maintain the doctrine and worship of the Church of England.

The anointing

The Queen changed into a simple white dress for the most mystical part of the coronation. She sat on the coronation chair, hidden from the congregation by a canopy, and was anointed with anointing oil.

Pocket tip ◉

The coronation robes and Crown jewels can be seen in the Jewel House at the Tower of London. Visit the Historic Royal Palaces website (www.hrp.org.uk) for more details.

The investiture

The Queen was dressed in the coronation robes and then presented with the golden spurs, the symbol of chivalry, a jewelled sword to be used for the protection of good and the punishment of evil and the armills, the golden bracelets of sincerity and wisdom.

The Queen sat in the coronation chair to receive the orb which reminded her that the world is subject to the power of Christ. The coronation ring of rubies and sapphires (often referred to as 'The Wedding Ring of England') was placed on the Queen's right fourth finger as a symbol of 'kingly dignity' and she was given two sceptres (see p.157).

The crowning

The most important part of the coronation took place when the Archbishop of Canterbury raised St Edward's Crown, the corona-tion crown, above his head and placed it on Elizabeth's head. A fanfare of trumpets rang out in the abbey and a great shout of 'God save the Queen' went up from the congregation. At the moment of the coronation, at the Tower of London a 62-gun salute was fired and the crowd outside the abbey started cheering. The Queen was then helped up (because of the weight of the crown and robes) and was placed on the throne where she took possession of her king-dom and received the homage of her people.

Pocket fact 🗲

St Edward's Crown was first used in 1661 by King Charles II. The original set of Crown jewels had either been melted down or destroyed by Oliver Cromwell after the English Civil War.

After the Archbishop of Canterbury the next person to pay homage to the Queen was her husband Philip, dressed in his naval uniform with his duke's robes of red velvet cloak and white ermine cape. Philip knelt before the Queen and placed his hand in hers and swore allegiance: 'I Philip, Duke of Edinburgh, do become your liege man of life and limb and of earthly worship; and faith and truth I will bear unto you, to live and die, against all manner of folks. So help me God'. Philip then touched the crown and kissed her cheek. Philip was then followed by the peers of the realm: the dukes, earls, marquises and lords.

Pocket fact 🗲

Prince Philip could not be crowned king because under the British monarchy the husband of the Queen has no recognised status, rank or privileges. The wife of a king can be crowned, as the Queen's mother was, becoming the queen consort.

At the end of the service the Queen changed back into her coronation dress and purple robe of state. Elizabeth wore the magnificent Imperial State Crown as she walked down the aisle of Westminster Abbey to the sound of the national anthem to emerge to the sound of cheering from the crowds outside the abbey. The Queen then returned to Buckingham Palace for the official photos taken by Cecil Beaton.

The return route from Westminster Abbey was planned so that as many people as possible could see their new Queen. The procession of 16,000 people stretched for one mile and took two hours to complete. The procession included all the members of the

Royal Family and guests including Queen Salote of Tonga, who won the hearts of the waiting crowd by refusing to put up the roof of her carriage in spite of the rain.

Appearance on the balcony

The Queen made the traditional appearance on the balcony of Buckingham Palace to wave to the waiting crowds in the Mall just as she had done with her father for his coronation. At 9.45pm she appeared again to turn on the 'lights of London', a specially constructed chain of lights cascading down the Mall lighting a huge cypher of EIIR on the Admiralty Arch. Lights lit the fountains in Trafalgar Square turning them silver and all the floodlights from the National Gallery to the Tower of London were illuminated.

Top ten facts about the coronation

1. *The Imperial State Crown contains four pearls traditionally believed to be Queen Elizabeth I's earrings.*
2. *The throne used during the service is now kept in the Garter Throne Room at Windsor Castle.*
3. *The recipe for the anointing oil contains oils of oranges, roses, cinnamon, musk and ambergris. In 1941 the last batch of oil was destroyed by a bomb but the pharmacy which made the oil had gone out of business. Fortunately the recipe was later found.*
4. *Polish artist Feliks Topolski was commissioned to produce a painting of the occasion for the Lower Corridor in Buckingham Palace. It was over 3 feet high and 98 feet long on 14 panels.*
5. *Coronation chicken was created for the guests who were given lunch. It contained cold chicken in a curry cream sauce.*
6. *Reporting on the coronation for* The Washington Times-Herald *was Jacqueline Bouvier, who later became Jacqueline Kennedy.*

7. *An Australian couple sailed from Australia in a small sail boat called a ketch to watch the coronation procession.*
8. *The Ministry of Food granted 82 applications for people to roast oxen, provided they could prove that oxen had been roasted on previous coronations. Ledbury in Herefordshire was one of the places granted permission.*
9. *Thirty cameramen were chosen to film the coronation in Westminster Abbey because they were slim and they had to fit into small spaces particularly above the organ loft.*
10. *Millionaire businessmen and country squires dressed as Buckingham Palace servants and helped take dignitaries to Westminster Abbey because there was a shortage of professional coachmen.*

♛ ROYAL EVENTS OPEN ♛ TO THE PUBLIC

Royal events that can be attended or watched by the public are the largest ceremonial events and include Changing of the Guard, Trooping the Colour and the State Opening of Parliament. They are historic occasions full of colour and tradition.

CHANGING OF THE GUARD

The Changing of the Guard is a daily ceremony that takes place on the forecourt of Buckingham Palace, where the old guard hands over the responsibility of the security of the palace to the new guard coming on duty.

Location
Buckingham Palace and Windsor Castle.

When
From May to July the Guard go into Buckingham Palace at 11.15am and come out at 12.00pm every day. This occurs on alternate days from August to April. During wet weather no ceremonial change takes place. At Windsor Castle the Changing of

the Guard takes place at 11.00am every day from April to July (except Sundays) and from August to March on alternate dates (except Sundays).

What happens

Buckingham Palace and Windsor Castle are guarded by the 'Queen's Guard'. The guard on duty will be from one of the five regiments of Footguards: the Coldstream, Grenadier Scots, Welsh and Irish. These guards wear the traditional red tunics and black bearskin hats and have guarded the sovereign since the court moved from Whitehall Palace to St James's Palace in 1689.

During the ceremony at Buckingham Palace the old guard exchanges duty with the new guard when the new guard marches out of Wellington Barracks into the palace accompanied by one of the Guard's military bands. At Windsor Castle the guard, accompanied by a Guard's band, marches through the town of Windsor into the Lower Ward of the Castle where the ceremony takes place.

Pocket tip ●
You can stand by the railings of Buckingham Palace to watch the symbolic changing of the keys but for the best view of the Changing of the Guard stand behind the flower beds in front and to the left of the palace.

CHANGING OF THE HOUSEHOLD CAVALRY

The Changing of the Household Cavalry is a daily ceremony where the guard going off duty hands over the responsibility of guarding the official entrance to Buckingham Palace to the new guard coming on duty.

Location

Horse Guards, Whitehall

When

11am on weekdays and 10am on Sundays

What happens

The Queen's Lifeguard is provided by the Household Cavalry, the oldest and most senior Royal Guard. The Guard dates back to 1660 when it was first started to protect King Charles II. The Lifeguards guard the official entrance to Buckingham Palace on Whitehall and are made up of two regiments, the Blues and Royals, dressed in their navy tunic and red plume on their helmet. The Lifeguards are dressed in a red tunic and white plume. The only person who is allowed to use this entrance is the Queen and members of the Royal Family and the guard on duty unless you have an 'Ivory Pass' (permission from the Queen).

The changing takes place on the courtyard at Horse Guards after the new guard has ridden down from their Hyde Park Barracks at Knightsbridge to replace the guard coming off duty.

Pocket fact 🚩

If the Queen is in residence at Buckingham Palace, there are four guards outside the palace in the sentry boxes and the mounted guard of the Household Cavalry consists of the 'Long Guard' of one officer, one corporal major (who carries the standard), two non-commissioned officers, one trumpeter and 10 troopers.

If the Queen is away, there are only two guards in the sentry boxes and the 'Short Guard' of the Household Cavalry has two non-commissioned officers and 10 troopers.

STATE OPENING OF PARLIAMENT

The State Opening of Parliament is an annual ceremony when the Queen formally opens the new session of parliament.

Location

Houses of Parliament, London

When
After the Easter recess at parliament or after a General Election.
The Queen leaves Buckingham Palace at 11.00am and leaves the
Houses of Parliament at 12.15pm.

What happens
The Queen gives a speech to open each new session of parliament
and sets out the government's legislative business for the coming
year. The ceremony takes place at the Houses of Parliament where
the House of Lords and the House of Commons are summoned
to hear the Queen's speech from the throne.

Pocket fact 🖼

*A member of the government is held hostage at Buckingham
Palace before the Queen leaves to ensure her safe return. The tradition dates from the 17th century when the relationship
between parliament and the monarchy was less friendly.*

Before the Queen leaves Buckingham Palace for parliament the
Queen's Body Guard of the Yeomen of the Guard search the cellars of the Houses of Parliament. This tradition stems from the
Gunpowder Plot of 1605 when five plotters including Guy Fawkes
smuggled 36 barrels of gunpowder through a tunnel into the old
Houses of Parliament. They wanted to blow up James I because
he had failed to restore the Catholic Church and had expelled
Jesuit and Catholic priests. The plot was discovered though and
the men executed, but since then the cellars have always
been searched.

The Queen's Body Guard of the Yeomen of the Guard

*The Guard was created by King Henry VII in 1485 at the Battle
of Bosworth and is the oldest military corps in existence in*

> Britain. It consists of 73 men who are former officers and sergeants of the British military. Their distinctive Tudor uniforms are very similar to the uniforms of the yeoman warders at the Tower of London except for the cross belts, worn from the left shoulder and they carry a sword and a halberd (a two-headed axe on a pole). Their role is purely ceremonial and they take part in a number of royal events including the State Opening of Parliament, investitures and summer garden parties at Buckingham Palace, the coronations, lying-in-state, and funeral of the sovereign.

The Queen travels in the Irish State Coach accompanied by Prince Philip along the Mall and down Whitehall, escorted by the Household Cavalry. The parade is led by a 100-strong Guard of Honour made up of the Footguards and accompanied by military bands with the route lined also by the Footguards. In front of the Queen, in the Queen Alexandra State Coach, is the Imperial State Crown (see p.156) and the Great Sword of State accompanied by senior members of the royal household. The Queen enters parliament through the Sovereign's Entrance.

The Queen is accompanied by senior members of the royal household including the Keeper of the Privy Purse (see p.129), Earl Marshall (see p.133) and Lord Chamberlain (see p.117) into the Chamber of the House of Lords. The members of parliament are summoned by Black Rod, who is responsible for security and access to the House of Lords. As Black Rod approaches the House of Commons the door is slammed in his face to demonstrate the independence of the House of Commons from the monarchy.

Pocket fact 🚩

The Queen has opened parliament every year of her reign except in 1959 and 1963 when she was expecting Prince Andrew and Prince Edward. At those times, the lord commissioners, headed by the Archbishop of Canterbury, carried out the Queen's duties and the Lord Chancellor read out the Queen's speech.

Black Rod knocks on the door three times with his black rod and asks the Sergeant-at-Arms: 'Mr Speaker, The Queen commands this Honourable House to attend Her Majesty immediately in the House of Peers'. The members of parliament proceed to the House of Lords to listen to the Queen's speech. The Queen then returns to Buckingham Palace in the carriage procession.

Pocket tip ◐

To watch the Queen's procession to and from the Houses of Parliament you can stand anywhere on the Mall or in Whitehall. To watch the Queen go into the Houses of Parliament and see the Guard of Honour and all the comings and goings stand by the House of Lords, St Margaret's Street. It is not possible to go inside the House of Lords during the ceremony.

TROOPING THE COLOUR

Trooping the Colour celebrates the Queen's official birthday. As mentioned above, the Queen's actual birthday is on 21 April but she also has an official birthday to celebrate her coronation in June 1953.

Location
Horse Guard's Parade, Whitehall

When
June

What happens
Trooping the Colour is a military parade where the colour or flag of the regiment is trooped or carried in front of the sovereign. The custom of Trooping the Colour (not Trooping of the Colour) dates back to the 17th century when the colours (flags) of a regiment were used as a rallying point for soldiers in battle and were trooped in front of the men everyday so they would recognise their colour. The ceremony was first associated with the sovereign's birthday in 1748 for King George III and became a permanent royal event by 1820.

Pocket fact 🛈

The Queen attended her first Trooping the Colour in 1947 as Princess Elizabeth when her father took the salute and again in 1951 when she deputised for her father. The Queen has attended every Trooping the Colour since she became Queen except in 1955 when there was a rail strike.

The Queen leaves Buckingham Palace in a carriage and arrives at Horse Guards at 11am accompanied by the Footguards regiments, the Household Cavalry and Royal Horse Artillery. The Queen takes the salute of 1,400 officers and men on parade from the five Footguards regiments, 200 horses from the Household Cavalry and the Royal Horse Artillery and 400 musicians from 10 military bands.

Pocket fact 🛈

The Queen used to take the salute on horseback until 1986 when her favourite horse Burmese (a gift from the Canadian Mounted Police) retired. The Queen now travels in a carriage and takes the salute from a dais.

The spectacle is truly awe-inspiring as the Footguards, wearing their red tunics and bearskin hats, carry out complicated marching manoeuvres accompanied by the wonderful stirring music of the military bands. Only one colour can be trooped and the Guard's regiments take it in turns. The Queen and procession then return to Buckingham Palace where the Queen and the Royal Family watch a RAF fly-past from the balcony.

Tickets to watch Trooping the Colour in seated stands must be applied for in January and February in writing and are allocated by ballot. Alternatively you can apply for the Colonel's Review (the rehearsal about a week before). Applications for both must be sent to Brigade Major, HQ Household Division, Horse Guards, Whitehall, London, SW1A 2AX.

Pocket Tip ●

You can also watch the procession on the day from the Mall or the ceremony from St James's Park from 9am but be aware your view may be obscured by the troops. The event is also televised.

THE GARTER DAY SERVICE

This event celebrates the oldest and most senior order of chivalry in England.

Location
Windsor Castle

When
Mid June

What happens
The Most Noble Order of the Garter was founded in 1348 by Edward III and was awarded for success on the battlefield and in tournaments. The Order of the Garter consists of the Queen, Royal Knights and 24 Companion Knights who are chosen personally by the Queen. The Order is given to those who have held public office, who have served the Queen personally or who are national heroes. The Order of the Garter is for life and any new knights can only be announced after the death of a knight. New knights are announced on 23 April, St George's Day, and are invested in June (usually on the Monday of Royal Ascot week) on Garter Day in the Garter Throne Room in Windsor Castle.

Pocket fact 🙚

Companion knights include ex-prime ministers Margaret Thatcher and John Major, Sir Ninian Martin Stephen who served as Governor General of Australia and Richard Luce, Lord Chamberlain to the Queen.

The garter regalia

The regalia of the Order of the Garter consist of the following.

- **The dark blue velvet mantle** (cloak).

- **The garter.** This is a dark blue velvet ribbon with a buckle and edged with gold with the motto of the order in gold letters. It is worn below the left knee by men and the upper arm by women.

- **The garter star.** This is an eight-point star with the enamelled Cross of St George encircled by the dark blue, enamelled garter.

- **The collar.** This is made of gold and consists of 24 interlaced knots alternated with 24 enamelled Tudor roses joined together with gold links. Suspended from the collar is a gold and enamelled figure of St George on horseback slaying a dragon.

- **The hat.** This is made of black velvet with a plume of white ostrich feathers and a tuft of black heron feathers.

The regalia are returned on the death of a knight. Following the investiture of any new knights, the Queen and Royal Family and members of the Order of the Garter have lunch in the Waterloo Chamber. After lunch the Queen, the Royal Family and the knights all dressed in their sumptuous garter robes proceed from the Upper Ward of Windsor Castle to St George's Chapel preceded by the Constable and Governor of Windsor Castle and the Military Knights of Windsor. After the ceremony the Queen, the Royal Family and garter knights return in carriages and cars.

Pocket tip ●

The procession is a public event and a limited amount of tickets are available. You can apply for up to four tickets from 1 January to 1 March by sending an email to garterday.info@royal.gsx. gov.uk.

THE THISTLE SERVICE

The Order of the Thistle is the highest order of chivalry in Scotland and is awarded for those who have held public office or have contributed to national life. The motto is *Nemo me impune lacessit* ('No one harms me with impunity').

Location
St Giles' Cathedral, Edinburgh

When
Every other year at the end of June or beginning of July

What happens
The Order of the Thistle was begun by King James VII of Scotland (King James II of England) in 1687. The knights are chosen personally by the Queen and are installed in the Chapel of St Giles' Cathedral following the announcement of their appointment on St Andrew's Day (30 November).

Pocket fact 🛈

The 19th-century Signet Library is the home of the Society of Writers to Her Majesty's Signet, the independent association for lawyers in Scotland.

The Knights of the Order of the Thistle wait in the Signet Library for the arrival of the Queen and Prince Philip in Parliament Square. Then the Queen and Prince Philip are conducted to the Signet Library and they all process into the Chapel of the Order in St Giles for the installation of any new knights. At the end of the service they go back into the Signet Library for a short reception followed by lunch at the Palace of Holyroodhouse.

Pocket fact 🎟

The service for the Order of the Thistle takes place during Holyrood Week, usually the end of June and beginning of July, when the Queen undertakes a number of engagements in Scotland including a garden party (see p.108), investiture (see p.104) and official engagements at the Scottish Parliament.

The regalia for the Order of the Thistle are a dark green velvet mantle (cloak) with a collar decorated with thistles and a badge with St Andrew holding his cross. The breast star is a cross with pointed rays between the arms of the cross and at the centre is a thistle surrounded by the order's motto.

Pocket tip ●

The public can apply for tickets in writing to the Scottish Government Protocol Unit, Area 2-J North, Victoria Quay, Edinburgh EH6 6QQ.

ROYAL ASCOT

Royal Ascot is a five-day flat race meeting of around 30 races. The Queen visits on the Tuesday, Wednesday, Thursday and Friday.

Location
Ascot Racecourse, Ascot, Berkshire

When
Third week in June

What happens
Royal Ascot is one of the premier flat race meetings in the country and is attended by the Queen and her guests. Ascot Racecourse was founded by Queen Anne in 1711 and today one of the races is called the Queen Anne Stakes in memory of the racecourse

founder. In 1813 parliament passed the Act of Enclosure to ensure that racing would continue on the site and the racecourse is now the property of the Crown Estates (see p.131).

Pocket fact 🎱

The Queen has attended Royal Ascot every year since 1945.

The origin of Royal Ascot is unsure as the first meet was in 1768 but it wasn't until 1807 and the introduction of the Gold Cup race that the event as we know it today took shape. Although the Crown Estates run Ascot Racecourse the Queen appoints 'Her Majesty's Representative at Ascot' to run the racecourse, along with the clerk of the course, a chief executive, trustees and non-executive and departmental directors.

Pocket fact 🎱

It has become customary for the bookmakers at Ascot to take bets on the colour of the Queen's hat!

The Queen and her guests occupy the Royal Box, which is level with the finish line. Royal Ascot week is one of the highlights of the summer events and entrance into the Royal Enclosure is gained by the sponsorship from an existing member who has attended in four previous years. The dress code is morning dress (tail coat and top hat) for men and a day dress for ladies. The Queen traditionally presents the Gold Cup, the Royal Hunt Cup and the Queen's Vase. The most popular day is Ladies Day, on the Thursday, when the hats take on a life of their own as the women try to out do each other with even more elaborate styles. The Queen has had over 20 winners at Royal Ascot.

Pocket tip ◉

You can attend Royal Ascot and if you time it right, it is possible to see the Queen drive through Windsor Great Park. For more details visit the Royal Ascot website (www.ascot.co.uk).

REMEMBRANCE DAY

Remembrance Day is a memorial to remember all those who have given their lives in service of their country.

Location
The Cenotaph, Whitehall, London

When
The second Sunday of November (and 11 November)

What happens
On the day before the service, the Queen attends the annual Festival of Remembrance at the Royal Albert Hall organised by the Royal British Legion, which provides help and welfare to all serving and ex-servicemen and women. The festival is a mixture of musical performances culminating in the release of thousands of poppy petals from the ceiling.

Pocket fact 🂫

The red poppy is the symbol of the Royal British Legion and the legion collects money in exchange for paper poppies leading up to 11 November. The poppy flower was adopted as the symbol of commemoration because the poppy was the first and only thing that grew in the aftermath of the First World War in Northern France and Belgium.

As the Queen is Head of the Armed Forces and a mother and grandmother who has had family members serving in the armed forces, the day is a particularly solemn occasion. On Remembrance Sunday the Household Cavalry, Footguard regiments and members of the armed services accompanied by Massed Bands of the Royal Marines, Army and RAF arrive at the Cenotaph. The Queen and Royal Family walk from the Foreign and Commonwealth Office on Whitehall to stand at the Cenotaph before Big Ben strikes 11am, the official time for the end of the First World War.

Pocket fact 🎖

The Queen wears a corsage of poppies on her coat and her wreath is made at the Royal British Legion poppy factory and has the inscription 'In Memory of the Glorious Dead' and is signed Elizabeth R.

A two-minute silence follows, marked by a gun salute by the Royal Horse Artillery and ending with another gun salute. The Last Post is then played by the buglers. The Queen, members of the Royal Family, leaders of the political parties and high commissioners from the Commonwealth all lay wreaths. This is followed by a short religious service and after a bugle call and the national anthem, the Queen and Royal Family depart. The war veterans who have attended the service march past with the salute taken by a member of the Royal Family.

Pocket tip ⚫

To watch the Remembrance Service stand on Whitehall.

GUN SALUTES

Gun salutes are fired by the King's Troop, Royal Horse Artillery or at the Tower of London by the Honourable Artillery Company to mark a special occasion. In London they are fired at Hyde Park at 11am, the Tower of London at 1pm and in Green Park at 11am for a state visit or the State Opening of Parliament and at noon for the Queen's Birthday Parade. They are also fired at Edinburgh Castle in Scotland, Cardiff and Hillsborough Castle in County Down, Northern Ireland.

The number fired depends on where they are fired. A basic royal salute is 21 rounds. If fired in Hyde Park, 20 rounds are added because it is a royal park. If fired at the Tower of London, 62 rounds are fired on royal anniversaries, 21 basic, 20 for a royal palace and 21 for the City of London, and 41 are fired on other occasions.

The salutes are fired on:

- 6 February (accession day)
- 21 April (the Queen's birthday)
- 2 June (coronation day)
- 10 June (the Duke of Edinburgh's birthday)
- The Queen's official birthday (a Saturday in June)
- 14 November (the Prince of Wales's birthday)
- The State Opening of Parliament
- Remembrance Sunday.

Salutes are also fired for royal births and when a visiting head of state meets the Queen in London, Windsor or Edinburgh.

♛ ROYAL EVENTS BY ♛ INVITATION ONLY

THE ROYAL MAUNDY SERVICE

As Supreme Governor of the Church of England the Queen attends a service at which she presents Maundy gifts to local pensioners.

Location
A cathedral or abbey in the UK

When
The Thursday before Easter Sunday

What happens
The tradition of the Queen presenting gifts on Maundy Thursday begins the Christian Church's celebration of Easter and has its roots

in the New Testament. The word 'Maundy' comes from the Latin word *Mandatum* meaning a commandment. It was at the Last Supper on the Thursday before his crucifixion that Jesus commanded the disciples to 'love one another' and he washed their feet. In the 16th and 17th centuries Tudor and Stuart monarchs would wash the feet of poor people as a reminder that they were there to serve their people and would distribute food and money. The ceremony stopped for 200 years in the 18th century and was revived by the Queen's grandfather George V in 1932.

Pocket fact

The service was traditionally held at Westminster Abbey but the Queen decided early in her reign that it should be held at a different location every year – a selection coordinated by the diocese (regional Church of England authority) who hosts Royal Maundy that year.

The Queen no longer washes anyone's feet and instead hands out Maundy coins. The original tradition is marked by the children selected from local schools, who attend the Queen wearing towels tied as sashes. The men and women who receive the money are chosen for their services to the church or community and the number chosen corresponds to the Queen's age. The Maundy money is presented in two purses, the design of which has not changed since Tudor times.

Pocket fact

The Maundy coins are sterling silver and although the Queen's profile on modern coins has changed over the years the Maundy coins have kept the first profile of the Queen used for coins in 1953. See p.149 for more on the Queen's profile on coins.

The red purse contains £5.50 in legal tender, and consists of a commemorative coin (in 2011 it celebrated Prince Philip's 90th birthday) and a 50p piece. The white purse contains the silver Maundy coins in pennies equivalent to the Queen's age. The purses are carried by the Yeomen of the Guard (see p.91) on silver gilt dishes (silver coated in gold) which date from 1661. The purses are then presented by the Queen to the chosen recipients.

Swan-upping

The Queen and the Worshipful Company of Vintners and the Worshipful Company of Dyers share ownership of every unmarked mute swan in open water but they only ring the swans on certain stretches of the Thames and its tributaries.

Every year the cygnets (young swans) are captured by the Queen's swan marker, royal swan-uppers and swan-uppers of the Vintners' and Dyers' dressed in their scarlet uniforms as they travel up the Thames from London in traditional rowing skiffs. When they reach a group of cygnets the cry of 'All up!' goes up to signal that the boats should get into position. The cygnets are weighed, measured and examined for any sign of ill health. They are then ringed and given individual numbers by the Queen's swan warden, a professor of ornithology at the University of Oxford's Department of Zoology and then set free. The data collected and reported helps to ensure a healthy swan population on the river.

Technically speaking only the Queen can eat swans, as anyone else would need permission to capture one.

INVESTITURES

Investitures take place when the Queen presents awards for services to the nation in commerce, industry, education, a charity or good cause or for bravery in the armed services.

Location
Buckingham Palace, Windsor Castle and the Palace of Holyroodhouse

When
25–26 investitures take place throughout the year

What happens
There is a long history of the monarch awarding honours as a mark of recognition for military service, gallantry or loyal service. In the past this was restricted to the aristocracy and the military but since the 19th century awards have been granted to a wider section of the population. Today the announcement of the recipients of the awards happens twice a year: at New Year and on the Queen's official birthday. The recipients are chosen from a list of names provided by the Queen's Lord Lieutenants (see p.64), government departments, local authorities, and educational and industrial organisations. Military and civilian awards for bravery are put forward by the Ministry of Defence and the government. The recipient is asked by the Cabinet Office if they would like to accept an award (although they are not told what it is, except if it is a knighthood).

Pocket tip ◉

It is possible to nominate someone for an award. You need to submit a nomination form obtainable from the honours website of the Cabinet Office, or obtained through writing, telephoning or emailing the Cabinet Office for paper copies. Go to www. honours.gov.uk for more details.

Once the Cabinet Office has received a nomination, the list is collated and the announcement is made. The Central Chancery of the Orders of Knighthood is responsible for organising the investitures. The department sends out the invitations and requests the names of the three guests the recipient is allowed to bring. The department is also responsible for laying out the insignia in the correct order for presentation.

Pocket fact 🔖

The Queen carries out around half of the investitures. The rest are carried out by Prince Charles or Princess Anne.

Around 2,500 people attend investitures every year and each recipient and guest receives an official souvenir programme. At each investiture around 100 awards are presented and there is a list of names with notes against each name so that the Queen knows exactly why they have been awarded and can make a personal comment to each one.

The investiture has the usual pomp and ceremony and the recipients and their guests enter through the Grand Staircase at Buckingham Palace on their way to the State Ballroom. The stairs are flanked by soldiers from the Household Cavalry standing to attention in full dress uniform. Gentlemen ushers (retired officers of the armed services) guide the people to their seats, while in the Musicians' Gallery a military band plays music. The recipients are lined up ready for their big moment.

Pocket fact 🔖

A knighthood allows the recipient to prefix their name with 'Sir' and the equivalent award for women is 'Dame'.

Awards have been given to people from many walks of life including sportsmen, actors, artists, politicians and soldiers and a lollipop lady who had escorted children across the road for 32 years. The Military Band will play something appropriate to the recipient when they are receiving their award. For example, when the singer Julie Andrews was made a Dame they played a song from *The Sound of Music*.

The Queen enters the room at 11am flanked by senior members of the royal household including her Lord Chamberlain (see p.117) and the Master of the Household (see p.124) and two Ghurkha orderlies (soldiers from the Nepalese branch of the British Army). The National Anthem is played and the Lord Chamberlain begins by announcing the name of the recipient and with a brief description of what the award is for. If it is an award for bravery then the entire citation is read out.

The recipients are lined up in an anteroom waiting for their name to be called. The awards are presented in order of seniority; the George Cross and Victoria Cross take precedence and are followed by those receiving a knighthood. During the investiture of a knighthood the person kneels on the velvet knighting stool and is dubbed (tapped lightly) on each shoulder by the Queen using the same sword her father George VI used. The badge or insignia of the knighthood is then either placed around their neck attached to a red and gold ribbon or attached to their lapel.

The awards

The awards are a small metal insignia usually in the shape of a cross with a coloured ribbon attached.

- *The Victoria Cross can only be awarded to a member of the armed forces for bravery, courage or gallantry.*
- *The George Cross is the highest award for bravery, courage or gallantry by a civilian or a soldier not in the presence of the enemy.*
- *The title of knight or dame is awarded for an outstanding long-term contribution in any field usually at a national level that was recognised as inspirational by their peers and demonstrates sustained commitment.*
- *The Companion of Honour award is awarded for an outstanding contribution to arts, science, medicine or government.*

- *Order of the British Empire which contains the CBE (Commander of the Order of the British Empire) and the MBE (Member of the British Empire). This is awarded for service to arts and science and public services and work with charities and welfare organisations.*
- *The George Medal is the second highest award for bravery, courage or gallantry by a civilian or a soldier not in the presence of the enemy.*
- *The Military Cross is awarded to members of the armed services for gallantry during operations against the enemy.*

The other awards are then presented in order of precedence. The Queen will have a brief few words with each recipient. The recipients are given a box for their award and then return to the Ballroom to watch the remainder of the investiture. After the last award is presented the national anthem is played again and the Queen and Lord Chamberlain leave the room.

GARDEN PARTIES

Attendance at the Queen's garden parties are by invitation only and recognise the contribution made by a cross-section of the public to the civil service, armed forces, a charity, organisation or the local community.

Location
Buckingham Palace and the Palace of Holyroodhouse

When
June and July and other special occasions including the Territorial Army's 100th anniversary in 2008 and 50th anniversary of the Duke of Edinburgh's Award scheme in 2006

What happens
Garden parties were started in the 1860s by Queen Victoria as 'breakfasts' even though they were held in the afternoon. In 1952 the Queen changed the number held from two to three and widened the guest list to include a broad cross-section of the

public. An invitation to a garden party is a recognition by the Queen and the invitations are decided from a list of names nominated by the armed forces, government departments, councils, diplomatic corps, charities and professional bodies. The majority of the names come from the Lord Lieutenants (see p.64).

The doors to Buckingham Palace open at 3pm to allow people to walk around the grounds as this is the only time the public have access to the whole of the 40 acres of gardens. The guests are formed into lanes to allow the maximum access to the Queen and other members of the Royal Family who are expected to attend. The Queen's Senior Gentleman Usher and his gentlemen usher assistants move down the lanes finding interesting people to introduce to the Queen.

Pocket fact 🚩

The gentlemen ushers try to find a cross-section of people from all walks of life and choose people who would not normally have an opportunity to meet the Queen. They find out why they have been invited and then tell them they are going to be introduced. They are then given a quick lesson in etiquette on how to curtsey and address the Queen.

At 4pm the Queen and Prince Philip arrive with other members of the Royal Family and the national anthem is played. They then move down the lanes stopping to chat and greet as wide a variety of people as possible.

The lanes are marked out by the Yeomen of the Guard (see p.91) and it is their job to make sure nothing untoward happens. In 2003 one of the guards rugby tackled the son of a teacher, who had been invited for his services to education, as he was about to step out of his trousers to streak in front of the Queen.

The Lord Chamberlain (see p.117) accompanies the Queen making the introductions. It takes about an hour for the Queen to walk the 250 yards down the lane of guests. At last the Queen gets to have a cup of tea with a group of selected guests in the royal tea tent and at 6pm the Queen returns to the palace.

Top ten facts about the garden parties

1. For each party at Buckingham Palace, 10,000 guests are invited and they drink about 27,000 cups of tea and eat 20,000 sandwiches and 20,000 slices of cake.

2. The buffet table is 400ft long.

3. At the garden party held at the Palace of Holyroodhouse in Scotland the 10,000 guests eat an average of 14 items including Scottish shortbread and Dundee cake, whereas at Buckingham Palace the guests eat an average of 10 items.

4. Originally guests came by themselves but the Queen changed it so they could bring a friend, neighbour or family member.

5. At one garden party there was a terrible thunderstorm and three girls who sheltered under a tree were struck by lightning. They were unhurt but their tights melted.

6. A record is kept of every guest invited as most guests are only invited once.

7. The invitation reads 'The Lord Chamberlain is commanded by Her Majesty to invite . . . To a Garden Party'

8. Non-British residents can write to their High Commission (Embassies of Commonwealth Countries – see p.58) to request one of the invitations reserved for each country.

9. The invitations are handwritten and guests also need a handwritten admittance card to gain entry.

10. There is a 'Black List' of people who are never to be invited to a royal function, and once a name is on the list it is very rarely removed.

CHRISTMAS BROADCAST

Location
Usually at Buckingham Palace but Windsor Castle and Sandringham are also used

When
Christmas Day

What happens
The first royal Christmas broadcast took place in 1932 and was given by the Queen's grandfather George V at Sandringham House. The early royal broadcasts were transmitted live on the radio and reached 20 million people as far away as Australia, Canada, India, Kenya and South Africa. It wasn't until 1939 that they became an annual event. The Queen's first broadcast was in December 1952 after her accession to the throne.

Top ten facts about the Queen's Christmas broadcast

1. *There have been 58 Christmas broadcasts.*
2. *The Queen uses the same desk and chair that her father and grandfather used.*
3. *The broadcast was first televised in 1957.*
4. *From 1960 recordings have been made of the speech and sent to the Commonwealth countries to allow them to be broadcast at local time.*
5. *The Queen has missed only one broadcast in 1969 because of a repeat showing of the documentary* The Royal Family *over the Christmas period.*
6. *In 1963 the broadcast was on radio only as the Queen was pregnant with her fourth child, Prince Edward.*
7. *The speech is recorded a few days before Christmas.*
8. *In 2003 the Queen broke with tradition and filmed the Christmas broadcast on location at the Combermere Barracks in Windsor.*

> 9. *The speech always contains a comment on events at home and abroad such as the assassination of John F. Kennedy in 1963 and the 50th anniversary of the Normandy landings in 1994.*
> 10. *The broadcast can also be downloaded from the British Monarchy's website (www.royalgov.co.uk) as a podcast.*

The Christmas broadcast is the Queen's personal message to her people and is one of the few occasions that she speaks without the advice of the government. The broadcast gives her an opportunity to speak to her people of recent events that they may be affected by, such as war in the Middle East, the destruction of the World Trade Centre in New York and the Falklands War, and of personal events such as the birth of her children and the 60th birthday of Prince Charles in 2008.

OTHER ROYAL EVENTS

- **The Royal Variety Performance**. The Queen and Prince Philip attend this annual evening of entertainment at a different theatre every year in aid of the Entertainment Artistes' Benevolent Fund.

- **Services of Thanksgiving**. These are held to celebrate a variety of anniversaries and commemorations either of national importance or personal events of the Royal Family including the Queen's 80th birthday, the Queen and the Duke of Edinburgh's silver, golden and diamond wedding anniversaries and the 300th anniversary of the building of St Paul's Cathedral.

- **Chelsea Flower Show**. The Queen attends the annual flower show held in the grounds of the Royal Hospital Chelsea in May as Patron of the Royal Horticultural Society.

- **Beating Retreat**. This military ceremony of music and marching by the Mounted Bands of the Household Cavalry and the Massed Bands of the Household Division dates back to the 16th century when the beating of the drums signalled the closing of the gates at the end of the day. The ceremony takes place at Whitehall in London on two successive evenings in June when the salute is taken by a member of the Royal Family. All proceeds go to service charities. For details on how to obtain tickets visit the Army website (www.army.mod.uk/events/events/3056.aspx).

Pocket fact 🔑

The Royal Windsor Horse Show is held at Windsor every May. It began in 1943 as a charity event with George VI as its patron. The Queen became the patron in 1952 and she attends the five-day event every year.

5

THE ROYAL HOUSEHOLD

The organisation that is required to ensure the smooth running of the Queen's private and public life is immense. The royal household comprises a highly skilled and organised group of workers who enable the Royal Family to function. The role of the royal household is to protect, promote and support the Queen and to ensure that the monarchy remains relevant in modern times. This chapter will detail which departments are responsible for ceremonial occasions, finance, the royal palaces and the different roles within the royal household.

Pocket tip ●

The Queen and Royal Family use the latest technology to promote and keep the public informed on all that is happening. You can keep up to date on the Royal Family by visiting the British Monarchy website (www.royal.gov.uk) or their Facebook, Twitter or Flickr pages.

♔ DEPARTMENTS OF THE ♔ ROYAL HOUSEHOLD

The royal household employs 1,200 staff, of whom 450 are funded by the taxpayer and the rest are volunteers. The household is divided up into various departments that are responsible for ceremonial occasions, finance, domestic arrangements, travel, royal entertaining, investitures, information and press office, and property.

Pocket fact 🛈

The royal household is spread over several locations: Buckingham Palace, St James's Palace, Windsor Castle and the Palace of Holyroodhouse.

The departments of the royal household consist of:

- the Lord Chamberlain's Office (not to be confused with the Lord Chamberlain)
- Private Secretary's Office
- the Master of the Household's Department
- the Privy Purse and Treasurer's Office
- the Royal Collection.

THE HEAD OF THE ROYAL HOUSEHOLD

The royal household is headed by the Lord Chamberlain, who is the senior official of the royal household and its nominal head. The Lord Chamberlain is appointed by the Queen from a list submitted by the prime minister and he is always a lord (a peer of the realm). The role is part time and he is responsible for chairing meetings of heads of the various departments, and is closely involved with senior appointments and ceremonial duties including state visits and the State Opening of Parliament. On ceremonial occasions the Lord Chamberlain carries a white staff and keys, the symbols of his office.

Pocket fact 🛈

The Queen abandoned the practice of having people walk backwards when leaving her presence after an audience. The only people who continue to do it are the Lord Chamberlain and Palace Steward at state banquets and the Lord Great

Chamberlain at the State Opening of Parliament. They keep in a straight line by following the pattern on the carpet while fixing their eyes on the Queen.

THE LORD CHAMBERLAIN'S OFFICE

The head of the Lord Chamberlain's Office is called the comptroller and is responsible for organising the Queen's ceremonial duties. The Lord Chamberlain's Office has several departments:

- the Central Office
- the Central Chancery and the Orders of the Knighthood
- the Marshal of the Diplomatic Corps
- the Royal Mews.

The Central Office

The Central Office organises all incoming and outgoing state visits (see p.71), funerals and royal weddings and all annual royal events (see p.81) including investitures, garden parties, the State Opening of Parliament, Royal Ascot and swan-upping.

Pocket fact 🎟

It was the responsibility of the Lord Chamberlain's Office to send out the 1,900 invitations to the Royal Wedding of Prince William and Catherine Middleton in 2011.

These ceremonial duties also require the Crown jewels, ceremonial bodyguards and the royal cars and horse-drawn coaches of the Royal Mews and therefore these also come under the control of the Central Office of the Lord Chamberlain's Office. The planning of these events has to be meticulous as there are always many elements to take into consideration and everything in the ceremony has to happen in the right place at the right time.

Royal warrants

The Central Office also issues royal warrants to those companies who supply goods and services for at least five years to the Queen, Prince Philip or the Prince of Wales.

The awarding of a royal warrant to a company allows them to use the relevant royal arms and 'By Appointment' label on their products, premises, stationery, vehicles and advertising. The Queen has awarded royal warrants to companies such as Clarins, John Lewis and Barbour.

The Central Chancery and the Orders of the Knighthood

The Central Office of the Lord Chamberlain's Office also oversees the Central Chancery and the Orders of the Knighthood, which are responsible for the awards given by the Queen at investitures and the appointments to the Ecclesiastical and Medical Households. The Ecclesiastical Household are the chaplains of the Queen, including those at St James's Palace, Buckingham Palace and Windsor Castle. The Medical Household consists of two physicians to the Queen one of whom is a homeopath, as well as other specialists including an orthopaedic surgeon and a dental surgeon.

Pocket fact 🛈

The Queen attends church every Sunday and when she is at Windsor she attends the Royal Chapel of All Saints in the grounds of Windsor Great Park. It also gives her the chance to meet up with those who live and work at Windsor.

The Marshal of the Diplomatic Corps

This department is the Queen's link with the heads of diplomatic missions (embassies and high commissions) of which there are currently 150. It is their role to arrange for outgoing and incoming ambassadors and high commissioners to be received by the Queen and invite them to the State Opening of Parliament, Royal Ascot, the garden parties and the annual Diplomatic Reception.

Pocket fact 🃏

1,000 guests are invited to the Diplomatic Reception held at Buckingham Palace in November. It is a high-profile affair with past prime ministers, the archbishops of Canterbury and York and members of the cabinet and their wives. All the ambassadors and high commissioners meet the Queen and Prince Philip and there is a buffet supper followed by dancing.

The Royal Mews

The Royal Mews is headed by the Crown Equerry and is responsible for the Queen's cars, coaches and carriages for state and official occasions. The Royal Mews contains all the ceremonial coaches and carriages that are used at royal events including royal weddings, Royal Ascot and the Gold State Coach.

Pocket fact 🃏

It is not unusual for successive generations of one family to work for the Queen. Martin Oates, the senior carriage restorer at the Royal Mews, is the fourth generation of his family to work there.

The Royal Mews also has more modern modes of transport used by the Queen, including her eight state limousines consisting of two Bentleys, three Rolls-Royces and three Daimlers as well as a number of Volkswagen 'people carriers'. The most instantly recognised are those vehicles which are specially built with larger windows and glass roof that allow as many people as possible to see the Queen. The Bentleys and Rolls-Royces do not have registration number plates and are built so that the Queen can stand up with her hat or crown on before getting out of the car. When the Queen travels in the car her own private mascot of St George standing over a slaughtered dragon is attached to the bonnet.

Pocket fact 🔲

The Queen no longer drives around London but still drives when she is staying at Windsor Castle, Sandringham, Norfolk and Balmoral. Prince Philip has his own private London taxi so he can travel around London incognito.

THE PRIVATE SECRETARY'S OFFICE

The Private Secretary's Office is responsible for the Queen's private secretaries, the Queen's equerry, ladies-in-waiting, the Press Office, the Correspondence and Anniversaries Office, and the Royal Travel Office.

The private secretaries

The most important people in the running of the Queen's official duties as Head of State are her private secretary, the deputy private secretary and assistant private secretary. The private secretaries are appointed by the Queen and are her right-hand 'men', organising her official duties at home and abroad and writing her speeches and messages. Their role is also to assist the Queen in her role as Head of State. The private secretaries are the line of communication between the Queen and the British government and the other 15 countries where she is Sovereign. They inform and advise the Queen on constitutional, government and political matters and deal with her official correspondence and correspondence with the public.

Pocket fact 🎱

Wherever the Queen is in residence there is always a private secretary on duty.

The equerry

The Queen's equerry is a senior officer who is on secondment for three years from one of the armed forces (if you see any pictures of the Queen on official visits, the equerry is the one in the military uniform at the Queen's side). The equerry's duties are to support the Queen in her private life and when she is carrying out her official duties. The equerry is part of a small team of staff who are responsible for the detailed planning and running of the Queen's daily programme.

Some famous equerries are:

- John Spencer, Earl Spencer, the father of Diana, Princess of Wales, who was equerry to George VI and the Queen

- Peter Townsend, who fell in love with Princess Margaret when he was equerry to her father George VI (see p.35)

- Vice Admiral Timothy Laurence, who was the Queen's equerry from 1986 to 1989 and is married to Princess Anne.

Ladies-in-waiting

The Queen personally appoints around 14 ladies-in-waiting (both men and women) who attend her on public engagements at home and abroad. They are usually the ones collecting the flowers and cards on the Queen's visits and always remain close at hand.

The Queen chooses either her friends or long-serving members of staff to be ladies-in-waiting as a reward when they retire. They are among the Queen's closest companions so it is important that they are easy in each other's company. The women and men chosen must be able to mix with all levels of society and many of them will speak a foreign language.

The post is unpaid but they are paid out-of-pocket expenses and they can be on duty from 7am to midnight if required. The ladies-in-waiting work a shift system and will stay wherever the Queen is in residence. The lady-in-waiting on duty at Christmas will always be included in the family festivities at Sandringham House.

The Press Office

The Private Secretary's Office is also responsible for the Press Office which is headed by the press secretary with a team of 13 people. The Press Office deals with the world's journalists and broadcasters and ensures that the Queen and Royal Family get the maximum amount of good publicity for their official duties and royal events. The Press Office also maintains the royal website, Facebook and Twitter accounts, deals with queries from the public, issues the Court Circular (see p.63) and makes public announcements.

The Press Office is headed by the press secretary, who will always accompany the Queen on high-profile overseas visits such as to the US and will brief the press on the itinerary and give them the text of any speeches the Queen will deliver to ensure maximum coverage of the visit. The Press Office reads the newspapers every day to check for any articles on the Royal Family; these are then listed and copies of the list sent to every department in the royal household and to the Royal Family.

Pocket fact 🚹

The 'rat pack' is a small number of the media who work for the mainstream news organisations. Their job is to regularly report on the Queen and the Royal Family.

The Correspondence and Anniversaries Office

This department deals with the huge amount of mail received by the Queen, which can be between 50,000 and 100,000 items of correspondence per year. The department is also responsible for sending out 100th birthday telegrams and other congratulatory messages for anniversaries (see p.162).

Pocket fact 🎟

The Queen has received over three million items of correspondence during her reign.

The Royal Travel Office

The Royal Travel Office organises over 600 trips per year for the Royal Family. The department is headed by the director of royal travel and organises flights, cars provided by the Royal Mews (see p.119) and the Royal Train.

Pocket fact 🎟

When the Queen travels, the 'brown bag' goes with her. It is carried by a member of the royal household and contains all the emergency essentials she may need including spare shoes, stockings and gloves. The Queen can use five pairs of gloves a day shaking all those hands!

Air travel

Due to the amount of official duties the Queen and other members of the Royal Family carry out both at home and abroad the most efficient means of travel is to fly. However, the Queen has ordered that no journey less than 50 miles should be taken by air to save money and to reduce her environmental footprint.

Air travel is provided by the RAF No 32 (The Royal) Squadron, whose primary role is operational duties but any spare capacity is offered to the Royal Family. The squadron flies BAe 146 and HS 125 jet aircraft and the royal household provides a Sikorsky S-76 C+ helicopter for shorter journeys. For longer overseas journeys the Queen and the Royal Family charter a Boeing 747. If the

Queen is travelling to somewhere that a 747 cannot land then the Royal Squadron will be waiting to take over.

Pocket fact 🔳

The Queen travels with several members of the royal household including the Queen's messenger, who will travel back to London with any messages of a sensitive nature that cannot be trusted to ordinary methods. The messengers carry special passports in red covers with the words 'Queen's messenger' on the front and the words 'Charged with Dispatches' inside.

The Royal Train
The Royal Train is used by the Queen, Prince Philip, Prince Charles and the Duchess of Cornwall, and other members of the Royal Family can use it with the Queen's permission. The Royal Train is used if a royal visit is to be over two days or if the weather is too bad for the helicopter to be used. The train is a distinctive maroon colour and has a modern office, sleeping, and dining and support cars. The Queen's saloon has a bedroom, bathroom and a sitting room and double doors that open directly onto the platform. There are individual carriages for the Queen, Duke of Edinburgh, Prince Charles and the Duchess of Cornwall that can be attached to the train depending on who is travelling.

Pocket fact 🔳

Since 2007, to make it more environmentally friendly, the Royal Train has been run on biodiesel made from recycled cooking oil.

THE MASTER OF THE HOUSEHOLD'S DEPARTMENT
The Master of the Household's Department is responsible for the smooth running of the Queen's palaces, castles and houses,

including all entertaining carried out by the Queen. This department is the largest with around 250 staff. The head of department is usually a retired air force, navy or army senior officer as they need to have the military attention to detail. The Master of the Household has two deputies: the Permanent Equerry to the Queen, who is responsible for all her private domestic arrangements, and the Deputy Master of the Household, who looks after all other household departments.

The Queen's dressers

The Queen's dressers are the members of staff who work closer to the Queen than anyone else. The Queen has a senior dresser plus four other dressers. Their job is to ensure that the Queen has everything she needs to carry out her duties. They are there first thing in the morning, several times during the day and last thing at night.

Pocket fact 🎀

The most famous dresser was the Queen's nanny Margaret 'Bobo' Macdonald who started as a nursery maid and served the Queen for over 60 years. Bobo also became the eyes and ears of the Queen, always keeping her up to date on the comings and goings of the staff.

The dressers are informed of the following day's programme of events so they can have all the necessary clothes, hats, shoes and anything else that may be required, such as jewellery. The Queen can attend up to five events a day and a different outfit can be needed for each event. The dresser also advises the Queen what to wear and will offer a selection of clothes. They attend all fittings for new outfits and accompany the Queen on foreign trips.

Pocket fact 🛈

Many of the household staff retain their historical titles such as Mistress of the Robes (the Queen's chief lady-in-waiting) which dates back to the 16th century and Yeoman of the Royal Cellars, who is responsible for the wine cellars, a title that dates back to the 15th century.

The Queen's pages

The Queen's pages are the senior domestic posts in the royal household and consist of three sets:

- Pages of the Backstairs (who work closely with the Queen)

- Pages of the Chamber

- Pages of the Presence.

The pages have usually worked their way up from footmen to pages through merit. The Pages of the Backstairs wait personally on the Queen in her first floor apartments and it is through the pages that access to the Queen is granted.

Pocket fact 🛈

The Queen commands a great sense of loyalty from her staff, and many of them work for her all their working lives. The Royal Victorian Order medal is presented to people who have served the monarch in a personal way and the Queen often awards this to long-serving members of her staff.

Where the staff live

Many of the staff live in the royal residences due to the unsociable hours that they work, with early starts and late finishing. Buckingham Palace is the only residence to have full-time staff, and the other residences are run with a skeleton staff except when the Queen is in residence, when the Buckingham Palace staff move with her. It is the responsibility of the Travelling Yeoman to organise the transport of the staff.

The household departments

F Branch: food branch

F Branch is responsible for preparing and cooking all the food for the Royal Family and staff and for state banquets, receptions and garden parties. F Branch consists of the Royal Chef and all his assistant chefs, kitchen porters, dining room staff, storemen and office staff. The chefs and staff also travel with the Queen when staying at Windsor Castle, Balmoral Castle and Sandringham House. The state-of-the-art kitchens at Buckingham Palace and Windsor Castle have all the latest hi-tech equipment.

F Branch is also responsible for all the washing up, and due to the delicate nature and historical value of the dining services, some of them which are over 200 years old, they are all washed by hand in rubber-lined sinks to prevent breakages. The silver gilt plates are hand washed and individually wrapped in cling film.

Pocket fact 🔲

The state banquets can have around 160 guests with six glasses each: that is 960 glasses to be washed by hand!

G Branch: general branch

G Branch organises and runs all ceremonial events and entertaining at home and on special occasions overseas. This branch also provides the staff for the ceremonial events including the footmen, under-butlers, Yeoman of the Glass and China, and gilt and silver pantries. G branch has no trouble employing staff, advertising in catering staff trade papers and through the palace website.

Pocket fact 🎗

It is the responsibility of the Yeoman of the Glass and China pantry to mark each item of china and glass in his book and to check it back in every time they are used. He also provides table cards at the functions so that guests know what china is being used and its history.

H branch: housekeeping branch

H branch is headed by the chief housekeeper and staff of around 30, including a deputy and assistant housekeeper and housemaids. The chief housemaid in turn heads around 20 maids, who do the vacuuming and dusting. The senior housemaid's job is to wait on the female members of the Royal Family, including bringing the Queen her breakfast tray. H branch is in charge of all laundry and linen, some of which dates back to Queen Victoria in the 19th century.

Pocket fact 🎗

The maids who clean the rooms at Buckingham Palace are given instructions how each room should be cleaned, in what order and how the precious items should be handled. They also walk backwards when vacuuming so that no footprints are left on the carpets.

C Branch: craft branch

C branch is mainly based at Windsor and make, maintain, restore and conserve the priceless items of furniture, art and interior furnishings. There are about 16 staff including cabinet makers, gilders, upholsterers, French polishers and clockmakers.

Pocket fact 🖼

Gilders apply a fine gold leaf or powder to furniture, stone, plaster or metal to give a fine covering of gold. The gold used on the furniture and interior surfaces of Buckingham Palace and Windsor Castle is 23½ carat gold. It is applied with a soft-bristled brush which the gilder brushes across their face to create static; this allows them to pick up the very thin sheets of gold.

The Central Office of the Master of the Household

The Central Office of the Master of the Household is in charge of the coordination, management and administration of all official events, including the guest list and seating plans. The Master of the Household's department is also responsible for the superintendents based at Windsor Castle and the Palace of Holyroodhouse and those who are in charge of their day-to-day running.

It is the responsibility of the Chief Housekeeper to buy the staff Christmas presents on behalf of the Queen. A list is circulated in March asking the staff what they would like and the value of the gift is based on the length of service. The gifts are presented to the staff in December in the Bow Room of Buckingham Palace and they always act surprised even though they have chosen the gift.

Pocket fact 🖼

One member of staff asks for parts of a particular china service and hopes to have collected the whole service by the time he retires.

THE PRIVY PURSE AND TREASURER'S OFFICE

The departments of the Privy Purse and Treasurer's Office are headed by the Keeper of the Privy Purse who is known as the

Treasurer. The Finance Department is responsible for the Queen's financial affairs from public funding and the Keeper of the Privy Purse manages the revenue from the Duchy of Lancaster (see p.61). The Privy Purse and Treasurer's Office is also responsible for the Personnel Office, Internal Audit (which ensures the royal household departments are providing value for money) and the information systems management and telecommunications section, which provides information technology and telecommunications to all royal household locations.

Pocket fact 🖾

The Privy Purse and Treasurer's Office covers the Queen's private Royal Philatelic Collection, one of the finest stamp collections in the world. It was started in the 19th century by Prince Alfred, the second son of Queen Victoria. The number of stamps has never been counted and the value is not known because some of the collection is so rare that nothing similar has come on to the market.

The Finance Department

The Finance Department manages the revenue received from public funding. As from 2011 and financial year 2013/14 the Civil List was replaced by the Sovereign's Grant. The grant will cover the same expenditure as the old Civil List covering all the expenses that the Queen needs to carry out her role as Head of State and Head of the Commonwealth. This includes all central staffing costs, official receptions, investitures and garden parties.

Pocket fact 🖾

Contrary to popular belief the Queen pays income tax and has done since 1992.

Travel expenses and building maintenance

The Sovereign's Grant will also replace the old Grant-in-aid, which paid all the travel expenses of the Royal Family and maintenance of all the occupied royal palaces including Buckingham and St James's Palace, Clarence and Marlborough House Mews, the residential and office areas of Kensington Palace, Windsor Castle, the Royal Mews and the Royal Paddocks at Hampton Court.

Pocket fact 🖋

In 2010 the cost of the Queen to the taxpayer was 62p per person.

The Sovereign's Grant is calculated as 15% of the profit of the Crown Estates which was £230.9m in 2010, so the grant would be £34.6m. Any savings made by the royal household go into a reserve fund to allow for years when the percentage granted may be lower than what is spent. The reserve fund will never exceed 50% of the Sovereign's Grant. A copy of the royal household accounts is sent to the National Audit Office for checking and presentation to parliament.

The Crown Estates

The Crown Estates are land and properties that were previously owned by the monarch but whose revenue was given to the government by King George III in 1760 in exchange for the government funding the monarch. Over the years much of the land has been given away. The value of the Crown Estate is currently £6.7 billion.

The Crown Estates own:

- *Regent Street, Regent's Park, St James's area, parts of Kensington, Richmond, Hampton and Ascot Racecourse*
- *358,000 acres of rural land*

- *rights to all naturally occurring gold and silver*
- *half of the UK's foreshore, including moorings and ports*
- *the entire seabed out to 12 nautical miles, including minerals*
- *27,000 acres of forestry*
- *the right to extract minerals (gravel, sand, stone, limestone etc.) from 285,341 acres of land*
- *140 salmon fishing rights in Scotland.*

THE ROYAL COLLECTION

The Royal Collection includes paintings, drawings and water-colours, furniture, ceramics, clocks, silver, sculpture, jewellery, books and manuscripts, prints and maps, arms and armour, and textiles which are held in trust by the Queen as sovereign on behalf of her successors and the nation. This basically means that she can never sell them. The collection dates from the restoration of the monarchy in 1660 but there are some older items belonging to earlier monarchs such as Henry VIII.

Pocket fact 🔲

Oliver Cromwell gave away or sold all of the items owned by the monarch when England became a republic after the beheading of Charles I in 1649. When the monarchy was restored in 1660 the Royal Collection was started again by Charles II.

The Royal Collection is self-funding – that is, it is funded by the Royal Collection Trust set up in 1993 by the Queen under the chairmanship of Prince Charles. Items from the Royal Collection can be seen in the royal palaces and residences and in the Queen's Gallery, which has a changing exhibition of items from the collection. Over 3,000 items from the collection are on long-term loan to museums and galleries in the UK and abroad.

Pocket fact 🎟

The Royal Collection contains some of the world's finest art and includes 40,000 drawings. There are 600 drawings by Leonardo da Vinci and 80 portrait drawings by Hans Holbein. There are over 7,000 paintings by artists such as Titian, Correggio, Canaletto, Rembrandt, Rubens, Van Dyck, Vermeer, Lely, Hogarth, Reynolds, and Gainsborough.

The Royal Collection also has a commercial arm which charges entrance fees to Buckingham Palace and Windsor Castle and runs the Royal Collection shops and online shopping. In 2011 the Royal Collection raised over £41m. The range of merchandise includes commemorative cups and plates of the wedding of Prince William and Catherine Middleton, DVDs, books, oven gloves, cushions, jewellery and even a 'God Save the Queen' lollipop!

Honorary royal household posts

- *Earl Marshal*. *A hereditary post held by the Duke of Norfolk, who officiates at the State Opening of Parliament and who is responsible for the accession and coronation of a new monarch.*
- *Lord Great Chamberlain*. *Another hereditary post responsible for royal affairs at the Palace of Westminster and also officiates at the State Opening of Parliament. The title is held by three families: the Marquessate of Cholmondeley, the Earldom of Ancaster and the Marquessate of Lincolnshire.*
- *Lord Steward*. *The holder of this role attends Buckingham Palace on ceremonial occasions such as state visits and banquets where it is their duty to present the guests to the Queen.*
- *Master of the Horse*. *The ceremonial head of the Royal Mews, who attends the Queen at the State Opening of Parliament and Trooping the Colour (see p.93).*

- **Poet Laureate**. *The post is held for 10 years and is chosen by the Queen from a list submitted by the prime minister. The Poet Laureate makes the decision whether or not to write poetry for royal events such as weddings. In 2011 the Poet Laureate Carol Ann Duffy wrote a poem for the wedding of Prince William and Catherine Middleton.*

- **Bargemaster and Watermen**. *The Bargemaster is responsible for 24 royal watermen who work on the River Thames manning tugs and launches. They attend the Queen on ceremonial and state occasions, acting as footmen on royal carriages, and transport guests to Greenwich and Hampton Court when needed.*

♛ THE QUEEN'S SECURITY ♛

The Queen is protected by a branch of the Metropolitan Police called SO14, known as the Royalty Protection. They are uniformed officers who wear ordinary dress when on duty and accompany the Queen on any public visits at home or abroad and at the royal residences in London and Balmoral in Scotland. The royal protection officers are trained by the SAS (Special Air Service) (a corps of the army) in firearms and driving.

Pocket fact 🛈

The security officers attend state banquets and other formal occasions where they have to wear morning dress – a morning tailcoat, waistcoat, and striped trousers for men and an appropriate dress for women.

The men and women of the security branch have to be able to mix with people from all walks of life as they attend every function that the Queen attends. New recruits shadow existing officers for about six months before they fully take up their duties.

Buckingham Palace has its own police station behind the Queen's Gallery.

Pocket fact 🖼

A policeman sits outside the Queen's bedroom every night.

All royal vehicles carry homing devices so that they can be tracked wherever they are travelling. When the Queen is visiting a local region, the local police will supplement royal security.

Some royal security challenges

- *In 1982 the Queen woke up to find Michael Fagan sitting on her bed. They chatted for 10 minutes, on the pretext of getting him a cigarette, before the Queen called a footman. Her policeman had gone for a cup of tea!*
- *In 1992 Kevin Macmahon broke into Buckingham Palace grounds.*
- *In 1993 anti-nuclear protestors scaled the walls of Buckingham Palace and held a sit-down protest on the lawn.*
- *In 1994 American James 'Fanman' Miller paraglided naked onto the roof of Buckingham Palace.*
- *In 1994 two schoolboys from Eton College scaled the walls of Windsor Castle and triggered the alarms.*
- *In 2003 Aaron Barschak scaled the walls of Windsor Castle dressed as Osama Bin Laden and gatecrashed Prince William's 21st birthday party and stood within feet of the Queen.*
- *In 2004 one of the campaigners for 'Fathers 4 Justice' (campaigning for better access rights to their children) climbed on to the famous balcony of Buckingham Palace dressed as Batman.*

♔ ROYAL RESIDENCES ♔

The Queen's royal residences are divided up into official royal residences and private estates. The official royal residences including Buckingham Palace and Windsor Castle are owned by the Queen on behalf of the nation so she can never sell them. The Queen's private estates of Balmoral Castle in Scotland and Sandringham House are owned by the Queen personally.

Pocket fact 🗝

The costs for maintaining the Royal Residences is astronomical as many of the buildings are huge and old. In 2009 the estimated cost for updating the heating systems and repairing the roof at Buckingham Palace and Windsor Castle was over £20m.

OFFICIAL ROYAL RESIDENCES

The official royal residences are Buckingham Palace, St James's Palace, and the Palace of Holyroodhouse, the residential areas of Kensington Palace, Clarence House and Windsor Castle.

Buckingham Palace

Buckingham Palace is the London residence and offices of the Queen and Prince Philip and the administrative headquarters of the royal household.

Bought by King George III for his wife Queen Charlotte in 1761 from the Duke of Buckingham, the palace was remodelled by George IV, who was responsible for its lavish interiors. The palace was enlarged by Queen Victoria, who added an extra wing (the one with the balcony) and she was the first monarch to use it as a home.

The palace has 775 rooms, 19 state rooms, 52 royal and guest bedrooms, 188 staff bedrooms, 92 offices and 78 bathrooms. The palace has its own post office, cinema, bank, doctor's surgery, telephone exchange and police station. Buckingham Palace has 40 acres of gardens with a helicopter pad, swimming pool and over 30 species of birds. The magnificent state rooms of the palace are used by the Royal Family for ceremonial and state occasions and in August and September they are open to the public. See the Royal Collection website (www.royalcollection.org.uk) for more details.

Pocket fact 🚩

A flag is always flown above Buckingham Palace. When the Queen is in residence the Royal Standard flies above Buckingham Palace and when she is not in residence it is the Union Jack.

St James's Palace

St James's is the senior residence of the monarch in London and it is to the Court of St James that ambassadors and high commissioners present their accreditation.

The palace was built on the site of an old leper hospital by King Henry VIII in the 16th century. In 1702 it became the official London residence of the monarch and has remained so ever since.

Today St James's Palace is used for official and ceremonial receptions. It also houses some of the royal household departments including the Royal Collection, the Marshal of the Diplomatic Corps, the Central Chancery of the Orders of the Knighthood and the Royal Watermen. The palace is the London home of Princess Anne, and the Queen's cousin Princess Alexandra. It is not open to the public.

Pocket fact 🚩

The monarch's accession and whoever succeeds him/her is announced at St James's Palace from the balcony overlooking Friary Court.

Clarence House

Clarence House is currently the home of Prince Charles and the Duchess of Cornwall and Prince Harry.

Clarence House was built between 1825 and 1827 by John Nash for the third son of George III, the Duke of Clarence. The house was then occupied by a number of members of the Royal Family. In 1949 it became the home of Princess Elizabeth and Prince Philip until she became Queen and moved to Buckingham Palace. The house was then the home of the Queen's mother Queen Elizabeth until her death in 2002. Prince Charles refurbished Clarence House and it became his official London residence in 2011.

It is possible to take a guided tour around the house, which is open to the public in August and September. See the Royal Collection website (www.royalcollection.org.uk) for more details.

Pocket fact 🔋

Clarence House would appear on the television news every year when Queen Elizabeth the Queen Mother would come outside on her birthday to greet the crowds.

Windsor Castle

Windsor Castle is the largest and oldest continuously occupied castle in Europe and has been the home to English monarchs since William the Conqueror.

In the 11th century, William the Conqueror built a mound with a keep and since then a number of monarchs have enlarged Windsor Castle so that today it covers 26 acres. Windsor Castle is the Queen's favourite home and, if she has no other engagements, she spends the weekend there.

In March/April the Queen moves to Windsor Castle for a month for Easter Court when she hosts 'dine and sleeps' where invited guests (usually politicians, sportsmen and church leaders) stay for dinner, bed and breakfast. For one week in June the Queen stays at Windsor Castle during which time she attends the service of the Order of the Garter (see p.95) and Royal Ascot. The wonderful state apartments at Windsor are as lavish as Buckingham Palace and are used for official ceremonies and state banquets. The castle is open to the public, and for more details visit the Royal Collection website (www.royalcollection.org.uk).

Fire at Windsor Castle

In 1992 a devastating fire broke out in the small private chapel in Windsor Castle. It was started by a spotlight that was left on, which set a curtain alight. The fire quickly spread through the ceiling spaces and the damage was horrendous. A third of the state apartments were destroyed and it took 200 firemen, 15 hours and one and a half million gallons of water to extinguish the fire. Fortunately many of the precious objects in the rooms had been removed while work was taking place.

It cost over £37m to restore the state apartments, which was paid for by opening Buckingham Palace to the public in 1993.

St George's Chapel

The 15th-century St George's Chapel is within the precincts of Windsor Castle. Ten British monarchs are buried there, including the Queen's father and mother, George VI and Queen Elizabeth (the Queen Mother), and Princess Margaret's ashes are also interred there. It was in St George's Chapel that the blessing of Prince Charles's marriage to the Duchess of Cornwall and the wedding of Prince Edward, the Duke of Wessex, and the Duchess of Wessex took place. St George's Chapel is open to the public and a ticket for Windsor Castle covers both places, but opening times are different. For more details visit the St George's website (www.stgeorges-windsor.org).

Pocket Tip ●

You can attend services for free in St George's Chapel. Evensong is sung every evening at 5.15pm by the wonderful choristers.

Windsor Great Park

Windsor Great Park is part of an old Norman hunting ground that stretches from Windsor Castle in the north to Ascot in the south.

The park consists of 5,000 acres of deer lawns, woods, lakes and huge solitary ancient oaks. There is only one public road that runs through the park, linking Windsor and Ascot. The park also contains the Royal Landscape made up of Savill Gardens (35 acres of laid out gardens and exotic woodlands), Valley Gardens (250 acres of landscaped garden and woodlands) and Virginia Water (a huge lake with surrounding woodland). For more details visit the Windsor Great Park website, www.thecrownestate.co.uk/windsor_great_park and www.theroyallandscape.co.uk.

Pocket fact ⚑

Windsor Farm Shop, Datchett Road was the brainchild of Prince Philip. It sells produce from all the royal estates and local producers.

Frogmore House and Mausoleum

Frogmore House, in the grounds of Windsor Castle, is the 17th-century country house of various monarchs but is particularly associated with Queen Victoria.

Frogmore House is no longer a royal residence but is used by the Royal Family for receptions. The house is beautiful with a picturesque lake and landscaped gardens. The mausoleum contains the tomb of Queen Victoria and her husband Prince Albert with their effigies on top. Prince Albert was 42 when he died; Victoria was 81 but her effigy is of a youthful queen. The grounds of Frogmore also contain the Royal Burial Ground, where members of the Royal Family are buried. It is not possible to visit this area but there is an information board with their names. Frogmore is only open to the public twice a year. For more details visit the Royal Collection website (www.royalcollection.org.uk).

Pocket fact 🎖

The Queen's uncle, the Duke of Windsor (Edward VIII see p.4), is buried at Frogmore and next to him is his wife Wallis Simpson.

Palace of Holyroodhouse

The Queen's official residence in Scotland was founded as a monastery in 1128 but is best known for the tragic Mary Queen of Scots, who was beheaded on the orders of Queen Elizabeth I in 1587. She lived in the palace between 1561 and 1567. The palace was the home of Scottish monarchs until the death of the child-less Elizabeth I in 1603. The next in line of succession was James VI of Scotland so the two monarchies were joined together under one monarch and he became James I of England.

The palace is used by the Queen and Royal Family for state ceremonies and official receptions and for the Queen's annual garden party (see p.108) and investitures in Scotland. The palace is open to the public. For more details visit the Royal Collection website (www.royalcollection.org.uk).

Pocket fact 🎖

In Scotland the Queen's ceremonial bodyguard is the Royal Company of Archers, dressed in their striking uniforms of dark green tunic with black facings, dark green trousers with black and crimson stripe, and a Balmoral bonnet (a type of beret) with the Royal Company's badge and an eagle feather. The company was originally formed as an archery club in 1676.

PRIVATE RESIDENCES

Sandringham House and Balmoral Castle are the private residences of the Queen and it is at these homes that she holidays at Christmas and during the summer.

Sandringham House

The house was purchased by King Edward VII as a healthy retreat whilst he was still the Prince of Wales in 1862. The prince decided that the house was too small so he completely rebuilt it in 1870. The house passed down from father to son and both the Queen's grandfather George V and her father George VI died here.

Pocket fact 🚩

There are several properties on the Sandringham Estate, including Park House, where Diana, Princess of Wales was born when her father Earl Spencer was Equerry (see p.121) to the Queen.

The Queen visited the estate regularly as a child and during the Second World War she lived at Sandringham with her sister Margaret. Today the Queen and other members of the Royal Family spend the Christmas holidays at Sandringham from a week before Christmas to the beginning of February. The estate surrounding the house has nearly 16,000 acres of farmland made up of arable farms, woodland, orchards and village properties. Sandringham House, Gardens, Museum, the Stables Tearoom and Sandringham Church are open to the public in the summer months. For more details visit the estate's website (www.sandringhamestate.co.uk).

Top ten royal Christmas facts

1. The Royal Family exchange Christmas presents on Christmas Eve.

2. The Royal Family give each other inexpensive joke gifts such as a plastic shower hat and singing fishes but the children have proper Christmas gifts.

3. Every year the Queen gives Christmas trees from the Sandringham Estate to Westminster Abbey, St Paul's Cathedral, St Giles' Cathedral in Edinburgh, Wellington Barracks in London and the Royal Hospital Chelsea.

4. On Christmas Day the Royal Family walks to the 11am service at St Mary Magdalene Church near Sandringham House.

5. The Queen and Prince Philip send out around 850 Christmas cards.

6. The Queen gives out around 1,450 Christmas puddings to members of her staff, pensioners, and the palace police force.

7. The Queen likes to add the finishing touches to the Christmas tree at Sandringham.

8. Dinner on Christmas evening is very formal with long evening dresses for the women and the men in dinner jackets, after which they play charades and board games.

9. The Queen's Christmas cards are signed 'Elizabeth R' for official cards, 'Elizabeth' for close friends and 'Lilibet' (her childhood name) for relatives.

10. The Duke of Edinburgh organises a large shooting party on Boxing Day.

Balmoral Castle

Balmoral Castle and Estate is the private Scottish home of the Queen located in Ballater, Aberdeenshire. Balmoral was purchased by Prince Albert for his wife Queen Victoria in 1852 but the castle was considered too small for the Royal Family so Prince Albert had it rebuilt in 1856. Like Sandringham House, Balmoral Castle has been passed down through the generations.

Pocket fact 🛈

It is traditional for the prime minister to spend the weekend at Balmoral on the first weekend of September when the Braemar Highland Games are held. The games are attended by the Queen and members of the Royal Family and celebrate traditional highland games of caber (a large tree trunk) tossing, stone and hammer throwing, dancing and a tug-of-war.

The Queen spends July and August at Balmoral and the first week of October. The Queen, Prince Philip and Prince Charles take an active interest in managing the 50,000 acres of the estate and in conserving and protecting its wildlife and outstanding countryside. Balmoral Castle is open to the public and there are walks and guided tours around the estate by the rangers. The house and grounds are open to the public from April to July. For more details visit the Balmoral website (www.balmoralcastle.com).

Top ten facts about Balmoral

1. The Queen is a keen country dancer and often dances with her staff even when they are not keen. Mr Meldrum, her gundog trainer, ran outside when he was asked to dance with the Queen and had to be tricked to go back inside where the Queen offered to teach him the Scottish country dance, the Gay Gordons.

2. The interior of the castle is very Scottish with tartan wallpaper, carpets and curtains.

3. Every day with the help of a footman the Queen catches the bats which are hiding at the top of the Great Hall with a net and releases them; only for them to come back the following day.

4. Prince Philip runs the Balmoral Estate and the sporting facilities of hunting and shooting. It is possible to rent holiday cottages on the estate and pay to hunt and fish.

5. The Queen breeds Highland Cattle on the Balmoral Estate and has had several male champions.

6. The Queen breeds Highland ponies, fell ponies and Haflinger horses.

7. The Queen rides most days to check on the Balmoral Estate.

8. When the Queen is in residence her piper plays for 20 minutes around the castle.

9. Thirty of the Queen's household staff accompany her to Balmoral Castle.

10. The life of the Queen is more informal at the castle, with barbecues cooked by Prince Philip and the washing up done by the Queen!

6

BEING THE QUEEN

There are many aspects to 'being Queen'. Her portrait appears on stamps and coins and there are endless pictures taken for special occasions and numerous portraits painted for anniversaries and ceremonial occasions. There is also a certain expectation about what the Queen will wear at ceremonial occasions and state and regional visits. What would a Queen be without her crown and jewellery? This chapter will describe who decides on the portrait that appears on our stamps, coins and banknotes and how they have changed over the years. The chapter will chart the Queen's changing fashion over her reign and describe some of the Crown jewels and her private jewellery. It will also describe the Queen's correspondence and reveal just what it means to be queen.

Pocket fact 🔋
The Queen's cypher of EIIR appears on more than half of the 115,000 red post boxes in the UK.

♔ STAMPS ♔

It was not until 1840 that a uniform charge for the posting of letters was introduced and the first adhesive stamp, the Penny Black, was printed. The stamp bore the image of Queen Victoria as it was felt that this was the most difficult to forge. The stamp with the monarch's head in the centre continued for the next 120 years until the introduction of commemorative stamps in 1965, where the monarch's head still appears but in the top right-hand corner. The Queen approves all commemorative stamps, such as those for Christmas.

Pocket fact

In 2011 a law was introduced stating that the Queen's head must be on all postage stamps in case the Royal Mail was sold.

When Princess Elizabeth became Queen in 1952 her image on British stamps came from a photograph by Dorothy Wilding which shows the Queen half turned to the viewer. In the portrait the Queen wears the George IV diamond diadem (see p.158), which was given to her as a wedding present by her grandmother, Queen Mary, and is the crown worn by Queen Victoria on the Penny Black.

Pocket fact

The Queen sat for the portrait for her first stamp as Queen on 26 February 1952, just three weeks after her father George VI had died.

The image of the Queen that appears on stamps today dates from 1965 when five artists were asked to submit 'renderings' (representations) of the Queen. Arnold Machin's design was chosen and the first stamps with the new design appeared on 5 June 1967.

The Queen's head is always white with different coloured backgrounds to denote the value of the stamp.

Pocket fact

The Arnold Machin design has been reproduced over 200 billion times making it the most reproduced work of art in history.

♔ COINS ♔

By AD800, coins regularly had the name of the monarch printed on them so the next step was to put a representation of the image of the monarch on the coin. This image on the coin was often the only time people saw a likeness of the monarch.

There have been four images of the Queen used on coins since 1953 and in keeping with the traditions established in the 17th century the monarch always faces to the right. The first image of the Queen was created by Mary Gillick in 1953 which shows the young queen wearing a wreath. This image appeared on all UK coinage as well as the coinage of many Commonwealth countries.

Commemorative coins

The Royal Mint issues commemorative crowns worth £5 in legal tender to celebrate significant events including the 40th anniversary of the Queen's coronation, her 70th birthday and her 50th wedding anniversary. These are legal tender but are usually just collected and not used.

For 2012 the Royal Mint issued the official Queen's Diamond Jubilee Collection, a set of 24 historic silver coins that chart the events, ceremonies and landmarks of the Queen's reign, such as the State Opening of Parliament with words spoken by the Queen on the coins.

The portrait was changed in 1968 because of the early introduction of the 5p and 10p leading up to the change in decimal coinage in 1971. As with the postage stamp, it was Arnold Machin's 1964 portrait of the Queen that was used. The wreath that appeared on the stamp was changed and the Queen wore the George IV diadem instead.

In 1983 Raphael Maklouf's sculpture was chosen from the works of 16 artists to be the new image of the Queen on coinage from 1985. Raphael Maklouf worked from a photograph taken by Lord Snowdon but for the clay bust that was to be photographed to go on the coin he was granted a sitting with the Queen. There was much criticism that the image depicted the Queen much younger than her 57 years but Raphael said he was trying 'to create a symbol, regal and ageless'. Two designs were approved by the Queen, one for circulating coins and the other for commemorative coins.

Royal remarks

'On television, you get this formal image but when she's relaxed and talking, she is very different, absolutely friendly, making jokes all the time – even mimicking people.'

Raphael Maklouf

In 1997 the Royal Mint produced a commemorative crown coin to celebrate the Queen's golden wedding anniversary. A new image of the Queen was produced for the new coin created by Ian Rank-Broadley that would combine with an image of Prince Philip on one side of the coin and the Raphael Maklouf image of the Queen on the other side. The new image was so impressive it was decided that it should be used on all coinage and replace Raphael Maklouf's image with that of the more realistic 70-year-old Queen.

Pocket fact

For the Queen's jubilee a new £5 coin shows the original Mary Gillick portrait on one side and on the other side is the image inspired by the new sculpture created for the Supreme Court Building in Parliament Square, London by Ian Rank-Broadley.

♛ BANKNOTES ♛

Banknotes were introduced in the 17th century but it wasn't until 1960 that the image of a monarch appeared on the notes. In 1946 the Bank of England had been nationalised and it was decided that the image of the Queen on the banknotes would emphasise its public ownership. The hand-engraved image was also a good anti-forgery device as it would be difficult to reproduce the picture of the Queen accurately.

In 1956 the Queen gave permission for her image to be used on banknotes making her the first monarch to appear on paper money as previously the image of Britannia had been used.

The image by Robert Austin appeared on the 10 shilling and £1, £5, £10 notes. Since 1960 five images of the Queen have been used. In 1964 a £10 note was issued with an image of the Queen by Reynolds Stone. In 1970 there was the newly designed £20 note with an image by Harry Ecclestone, (the bank's first full-time designer) and in 1991 a newly designed £5 note with an image by Roger Withington appeared. The Queen's image is also in the watermark of the paper so that if you hold any notes up to the light you will see her image.

Top ten facts about the Queen's image

1. The most used image of the Queen is Arnold Machin's, which is of her wearing the George IV diadem.
2. The Queen and members of the Royal Family are the only living people allowed to appear on commemorative stamps.
3. The Queen's image first appeared on a postage stamp in Newfoundland, Canada, in 1932 when she was six years old. She also appeared on the Canadian $20 note in 1934 aged eight.
4. The Queen appears on the currency and commemorative coins of 33 countries, dependencies, former colonies and

overseas territories including Australia, New Zealand, Ascension Islands (commemorative) and Cayman Islands.

5. The Queen has previously appeared on the currency or commemorative coins of 40 countries that were formerly part of the British Empire including Barbados (commemorative), British East Africa, Cyprus and South Africa.

6. The Queen has appeared on more currencies than any other person, living or dead.

7. A total of 26 portraits of the Queen have been used on various currencies and coins.

8. Before she became Queen, the Queen's image was used on 28 stamps from 11 Commonwealth countries.

9. The Queen has also appeared on the stamps of non-Commonwealth countries such as Iran, Ethiopia and Brazil.

10. In 2012 the National Portrait Gallery will bring together 60 of the most notable and significant images of the Queen including portraits, photographs and press images in an exhibition called 'The Queen: Art and Image' that will be shown in London, Edinburgh and Cardiff.

♔ CLOTHES ♔

The public image that the Queen portrays has been carefully thought out and maintained throughout her reign. The Queen's image has changed over the years as she has matured but with limitations as she must always be easily seen in a crowd.

Pocket fact 🛈

The Queen never wears dark colours as they always photograph as black. Most of her designers prefer the Queen in daffodil yellow and periwinkle blue as those colours bring out the colour of her eyes.

At state and official occasions there is the expectation that she will look like a Queen dressed in elaborate dresses with a crown and spectacular diamonds. However, the most important element of the designs for the Queen's outfits is comfort. It would be highly impractical for her to dress as a Queen when off-duty. So on holiday in Balmoral in the summer months she is more likely to be found in a tweed skirt, headscarf and sensible shoes.

The Queen's first designer was Norman Hartnell, who designed her wedding dress in 1947 (see p.15) and her coronation dress. In 1953, when the Queen embarked on her first royal tour, it was very important that her outfits reflected her youth and her status as Head of State and at the time the ruler of much of the free world, but, most importantly, were stunning! Norman Hartnell's designs were constrained as many of the dresses needed to incorporate emblems, colours or flowers of the countries the Queen was visiting. In Ethiopia the Queen wore bright green (one of the colours of their national flag) and for the opening of the Montreal Olympics in 1976, the Queen's turquoise dress was embroidered with stylised rings reflecting the Olympic rings.

Pocket fact 🎁

In 2006 when visiting the exhibition of 80 of her gowns, the Queen remarked how heavy some of the bead-encrusted and heavily embroidered dresses were to wear.

The Queen began to use Hardy Amies as one of her designers in 1955. Hardy Amies was known for his outstanding tailoring and was responsible for many of the Queen's elegant designs, including a beautifully ivory duchesse satin dress covered in lace in gold and silver thread worn for the opening of the Maltese Parliament in 1967.

In 1970 the Queen asked Ian Thomas, who had been an assistant designer to Norman Hartnell, to design for her. For the Queen's tour to the Caribbean in 1985 Ian Thomas designed a number of evening and day dresses including a stunning, bright yellow dress with iridescent white and yellow sequins embroidered in a pattern that gave the impression of raindrops.

Pocket fact 🎀

The male designers never measure the Queen themselves. This is always done by one of the Queen's dressers (see p.125) or the designer's assistants.

When Ian Thomas died, his assistant Maureen Rose started to design dresses for the Queen. She designed the dress for the Queen's Golden Jubilee dinner for European sovereigns at Windsor Castle in 2002. The ivory embroidered dress took four seamstresses 600 hours to make. It was Maureen Rose's boast that no sewing machine ever touched a dress made for the Queen as every one was finished by hand.

Between 1988 and 1996 the Queen used John Anderson as one of her designers and when he died his business partner Karl Ludwig Rehse took over. Today, one of the Queen's designers is Stewart Parvin, who designed the beautiful pink dress and coat she wore at her granddaughter Zara Phillips' wedding, as well as Zara's wedding dress.

The designers all have to work with the Queen's milliners so that the hats match the dresses. The Queen's favourite milliners include Frederick Fox, Phillip Somerville, Marie O'Regan and Rachel Trevor-Morgan.

Pocket fact 🎀

The Queen always wears gloves as they prevent her hands becoming sore from constantly shaking hands with people.

THE QUEEN'S HANDBAGS

One of the most enduring images of the Queen is her handbag, which she carries everywhere. Here are some top facts about the Queen's handbag.

- There are treats for the corgis in the bag.

- The Queen is never without her handbag, even indoors and during the weekly audience with the prime minister.

- The handbags are usually black, regardless of the colour of her outfit. However, for Prince William's wedding her handbag was cream coloured.

- The bags are made by Launer of London, which has a royal warrant.

- The Queen keeps mints in the bag in case she gets a tickly throat.

- The Queen does not carry money, credit cards or car keys.

- On walkabouts the Queen holds her handbag on one side to signal to the lady-in-waiting that she wants to move on.

- There is an S-shaped hook in the bag which allows the Queen to hook her bag on the edge of a table.

- There is sometimes a camera in the bag as the Queen is a keen photographer.

- In 2004 as a joke the Queen opened her bag in front of photographers knowing how keen they would be to find out what was in her bag and revealed a purse, even though she carries no money.

♛ JEWELLERY ♛

The Queen has two collections of jewellery, the Crown jewels, which belong to her as a monarch, and her private collection. The Crown jewels are the greatest working Crown jewels in the world and cannot be sold as they are held in trust. The history of the

Crown jewels goes back to the oldest piece in the collection, the Anointing Spoon (see p.85) which dates from the 12th century. The majority of the Crown jewels date from the reign of King Charles II and the restoration of the monarchy in 1661. The highlights of the Crown jewels are St Edward's Crown, the Imperial State Crown and the Sovereign's Sceptres.

Pocket tip ◉

The wonderful and magnificent Crown jewels are on display in the Jewel House at the Tower of London. For more details visit the Historic Royal Palaces website (www.hrp.org.uk/ TowerOfLondon).

ST EDWARD'S CROWN OR CORONATION CROWN

The St Edward's Crown or coronation crown is only ever used at the coronation. The crown is a symbol of the monarch's right to rule and once their right to be the monarch has been confirmed by a coronation the crown is not used again. In the last 900 years there have been two St Edward's crowns, one that may have belonged to Edward the Confessor in the 11th century and was destroyed by Oliver Cromwell and the current crown that dates from King Charles II in 1661. The crown is made of solid gold and is decorated with 440 precious and semi-precious stones.

Pocket fact 🛡

Prior to the Queen's coronation she sat at her desk wearing St Edward's Crown to become accustomed to the weight of 2.23 kilograms.

IMPERIAL STATE CROWN

The most spectacular crown is the Imperial State Crown which the Queen wears for the State Opening of Parliament and other state occasions as the symbol of royal authority. The Imperial State Crown is also worn at the end of the coronation (see p.86). The Imperial Crown was made because the coronation crown could not be removed from Westminster Abbey (where it was originally kept) and so a crown had to be made for all state occasions. The state crown has always been more elaborate than the coronation crown and is set with a greater number of larger gems.

Pocket fact 🎩

The Imperial State Crown sparkles and glistens with its 2,868 diamonds, 273 pearls, 17 sapphires, 11 emeralds and five rubies.

Whereas other crowns were often set with hired gems when the Imperial State Crown was remade in 1937, for the Queen's father, George VI, it was set with a permanent set of stones and so contains the most historic stones. These include St Edward's sapphire, which sits at the top of the crown in the centre of a cross, the large and beautiful drop-shaped pearls, which hang from the arches of the crown and the Black Prince's Ruby, which belonged to Edward, the Prince of Wales (also known as the Black Prince). The most spectacular cushion-cut diamond of 317 carats, the Cullinan II, sits at the front of the crown.

Pocket fact 🎩

The arches of the Imperial State Crown were lowered for the Queen by about an inch to give a more feminine appearance to the crown and because she is quite small (only 5 feet 4 inches or 1.63 metres), the crown would have looked enormous otherwise.

THE SOVEREIGN'S SCEPTRES

There are several Sovereign's Sceptres in the Crown jewels but only two were used at the Queen's coronation. The Sovereign's Sceptres are long gold poles decorated on the top with either a dove symbolising justice and mercy or a cross to symbolise royal power of command. The Sovereign's Sceptre with Cross was made in 1661 for King Charles II and was remodelled in 1910 to incorporate the magnificent and stunning 536-carat, pear-shaped Cullinan I diamond (about the size of a chicken egg), also known as the First Star of Africa. The Cullinan I has the four most important attributes of a diamond: cut, colour, clarity and carats, making it the largest top-quality diamond in the world.

Cullinan diamond

The Cullinan diamond was found in the Premier Mines in South Africa and was named after the owner, Sir Thomas Cullinan. The uncut diamond weighed 3,025 carats (605 grams, about the size of a cricket ball) and was the largest diamond ever found. The government of the Transvaal (South Africa) purchased it and gave it to King Edward VII as a present. The diamond was cut in Amsterdam and the Cullinan I and II were given to Edward VII and the remaining stones Cullinan III–IX, 96 splinters and nine carats of stones were used as payment to Asscher, which cut the huge stone.

Edward VII purchased Cullinan VI from Asscher in 1909 as a present for his wife, Queen Alexandra, and in 1911 the remaining stones were purchased by the Transvaal government as a gift for the Queen's grandmother Queen Mary. Cullinan I was set in the Sovereign's Sceptre and Cullinan II in the Imperial State Crown. The remaining stones are in the Queen's private collection.

GEORGE IV DIADEM

One of the most familiar crowns is the George IV diadem (a type of crown) that was in the private collection of Queen Victoria. However, when she died, it was stipulated in her will that this was one of the pieces that was to be considered as belonging to the Crown and should be worn by right by any future queens, making it part of the Crown jewels.

The diadem was originally worn by King George IV at his coronation over a large black, broad brimmed 'Spanish hat'. The diadem was worn by the Queen at the beginning of her coronation and is worn to and from the State Opening of Parliament and is familiar to everyone as it appears on stamps and coins.

Pocket fact

The diadem has 1,333 diamonds and 169 pearls along its base and incorporates the national symbols of English roses, Irish shamrocks and Scottish thistles.

PRIVATE JEWELLERY COLLECTION

The Queen's stunning private jewellery collection is made up of pieces she has inherited from her mother and grandmother, pieces she has purchased and pieces she has been given as gifts.

Pearls

Although the Queen has this magnificent collection she is more often seen wearing either a two- or three-string set of pearls. The two-string set is known as the 'Queen Anne and Queen Caroline Pearls' and was given to her as a wedding present in 1947 by her father George VI and her mother Queen Elizabeth. The three-string set of pearls was given to the Queen by her grandfather George V on the occasion of his silver jubilee in 1935.

Pocket fact

The Queen's grandmother, Queen Mary, loved jewellery and is pictured in 1911 wearing seven rows of diamonds as a collar. Queen Mary gave many pieces to the Queen on her wedding day in 1947 and left her the rest in her will when she died.

The Girls of Great Britain Tiara

This tiara is also known as 'Granny's tiara' as it was given to the Queen by her grandmother Queen Mary on the Queen's wedding day. The tiara is a familiar image as the Queen is wearing it on £5, £10, £20 and £50 notes. The tiara was purchased as a wedding gift for Queen Mary by the Girls of Great Britain and Ireland in 1893. The tiara is in two parts with a small lozenge diamond bandana and a diamond scroll-shaped tiara with festoons.

For her 'something borrowed' at her wedding, the Queen wore her grandmother, Queen Mary's, Diamond Fringe tiara which Queen Mary had given to the Queen's mother. The tiara (which can also be worn as a necklace) was made for Queen Mary in 1919 from diamonds bought by Queen Victoria as a wedding present for Queen Mary in 1893. It was also worn by Princess Anne for her wedding to Mark Phillips in 1973.

The Cartier 'Halo' tiara

This tiara was given to the Queen on her 18th birthday by her mother Queen Elizabeth. The tiara was purchased by the Queen's father when he was still Duke of York (see p.3) for his wife the Duchess of York (later the Queen Elizabeth). The tiara is in the form of 16 graduated scrolls with 739 brilliants (diamonds cut in such a way to maximise their brilliance) and 149 baton-shaped diamonds. This tiara was Catherine Middleton's 'something borrowed' on her wedding day in 2011.

Pocket fact 🛡

The 'Maple Leaf' brooch worn by the Duchess of Cambridge on her first royal tour in 2011 was lent to her by the Queen. In 1951 when the Queen first visited Canada the same brooch was lent to her by her mother Queen Elizabeth who had been given it as a gift when she first visited Canada in 1939.

♔ CORRESPONDENCE ♔

The Queen receives around 300 letters a day, which are opened by the Correspondence Office within the Private Secretary's Office (see p.120). The rule is that letters must be answered by return. The letters are sorted and sent to the Queen's desk where she will select a number of letters to read and tell her staff how she wants them answered. The majority of the letters will be answered directly by her ladies-in-waiting or the Private Secretary's Office.

The Queen receives a wide range of correspondence, from birthday cards to correspondence from people who have tried every other organisation with their problem and have written to the Queen asking for help.

Vital statistics of the Queen's correspondence

- The Queen receives 3,000 birthday cards per year.

- For the Queen's 80th birthday she received 30,000 birthday cards. The largest was around a metre wide by one-and-half metres long and was made by children from Meonstoke Church of England Infants School in Meonstoke, Hampshire.

- The Queen receives lots of birthday cards from children, some beautifully decorated with pasta, tinsel but the most popular design is crowns and corgis.

- The Queen receives cards that sing happy birthday which drives the corgis mad.

- The Queen often receives party invitations from children.

- People send letters asking 'where to buy a corgi'.

- The Queen also receives wedding invitations – they would be surprised if she said yes!

- The Queen receives letters from the public telling her how much they have enjoyed their visit to Buckingham Palace.

- Personal letters from friends and family members have a letter code on the envelope so that her staff knows that the letters are private.

- The Queen has received more than three million items of correspondence during her reign.

- If you want to write to the Queen you can open the letter with 'Madam' and finish it with 'I have the honour to be, Madam, Your Majesty's humble and obedient servant'.

- You should address any letters to Her Majesty The Queen, Buckingham Palace, London SW1A 1AA.

CONGRATULATORY MESSAGES

Every year the Queen sends congratulatory messages to people for a number of occasions in the UK and her realms and UK overseas territories. The messages are sent out by the Anniversaries Office, which is part of the Private Secretary's Office (see p.120) at Buckingham Palace. The tradition of sending out congratulatory messages for those celebrating their 100th birthday and 60th wedding anniversary was started by King George V in 1917.

Regular congratulatory messages include:

- 100th birthday and 105th birthday and every year thereafter

- diamond (60th), 65th, platinum (70th) wedding anniversaries and every year thereafter.

Pocket fact 🂡

The Queen sent an official congratulatory message to her mother on her 100th birthday in 2000.

Top ten congratulatory messages facts

1. In 1952 there were only 3,000 congratulatory messages for wedding anniversaries and birthdays, but now that people are living longer there are over 9,000 for 100th birthdays and over 26,500 for diamond weddings.
2. The oldest person to receive a message was a Canadian man who was 116 in 1984. The oldest British person was a woman who was 115.
3. One couple has received five cards: for their 60th and 70th wedding anniversaries, their 100th birthdays and the man's 105th birthday.
4. Some periods of the year are busier for wedding anniversary cards because people like to marry during the bank holidays of Easter and spring.
5. In 2005 more diamond wedding anniversary cards were sent out than the previous year as it was 60 years since the war ended, which meant many soldiers had come back and married.
6. The Queen has sent out over 110,000 telegrams and messages to centenarians during her reign.
7. The Queen has sent out over 520,000 telegrams and messages to couples celebrating their diamond wedding anniversary in the UK and Commonwealth.
8. The Queen does not just send messages for birthdays and wedding anniversaries. She sent a micro-filmed message of congratulations to the astronauts of Apollo 11 for when they landed on the moon on 21 July 1969. The message was deposited in a metal container on the moon.
9. In 1997 on the occasion of the Queen's golden wedding anniversary she sent messages to everyone also celebrating their golden wedding anniversary. In 2007 when the Queen celebrated her diamond wedding anniversary both she and Prince Philip sent messages to 18,000 couples in

Britain also celebrating their diamond wedding anniversary in that year.

10. The Queen's signature has appeared on every card since 1999 (before this the telegram or telemessage did not require a signature).

The messages were originally sent by telegram but these were discontinued in 1982 and replaced by a card with an image of a royal residence or the Queen and containing a personalised message. The messages are delivered by normal post but are placed inside a special envelope. The image on the card is changed every five years so that those people receiving more than one don't get a duplicate. The message is not made public so that it remains a surprise for the recipient and the wording is changed so that it is different for those receiving more than one message.

Pocket tip ●

The congratulatory messages are not sent out automatically. Visit the British Monarchy website (www.royal.gov.uk) to apply for congratulatory messages for wedding anniversaries. Simply Click on the link for 'anniversary messages' and follow the instructions on filling out an application.

♔ A TYPICAL DAY FOR ♔ THE QUEEN

The Queen's diary can be planned over a year ahead as there are so many elements to be taken into consideration. For a state visit, all the invitations to diplomats, heads of government departments and guests would have to be sent out early to ensure their attendance. For the Queen's Diamond Jubilee the details were issued in June 2011, a full year before the celebrations took place. The Queen's staff has to be aware of any up and coming events that the Queen may have to attend such as the celebrations of the Battle of Trafalgar in 2005 or the London Olympics in 2012 as they can often be planning 10 years in advance.

Although the Queen undertakes a variety of duties every day, a typical day can look like the following.

MORNING

The Queen's morning begins at her desk scanning the newspapers and reading correspondence. The Queen receives over 200 letters a day, some will be answered by her staff but a selection will be answered by her personally. The Queen will then speak to each of her private secretaries separately, who present her with official papers and documents containing information from Commonwealth and foreign representatives, cabinet documents, telegrams, letters and her red boxes (see p.68 for more details).

Pocket fact 🎟

The Queen's breakfast tray consists of white toast, butter, jam and tea.

A number of audiences (meetings) will take place with overseas ambassadors, senior members of the British and Commonwealth armed forces, English bishops and judges on their appointment and retirement. These meetings normally take about 20 minutes. If there is an investiture it will begin at 11 o'clock and last for about an hour.

AFTERNOON

The Queen will lunch privately or there will be an informal lunch for invited guests, which takes place every few months.

The Queen will often undertake public engagements in the afternoon. If the engagement is outside the London area, she will use a helicopter or RAF aircraft to travel. These visits can include schools, hospitals, factories, sheltered accommodation for elderly people, hostels for the homeless and local community schemes in inner-city areas. On some of these visits she will be accompanied by Prince Philip but often they carry out public engagements separately so more can be covered. The afternoon may end with the Queen meeting with the Privy Council (see p.69).

Pocket fact ☒

The Queen carries out over 430 engagements a year to make speeches, open events and buildings and unveil plaques.

EVENING

At 7.30pm every evening the report of the day's parliamentary proceedings will arrive and the Queen will always read it the same evening. There will be evening public engagements consisting of film premieres, concerts or charitable events of organisations of which she is patron.

Pocket fact ☒

The Queen is a patron of over 600 charities. Visit the charities and patronages database on the British Monarchy website to access information on the Queen's patronage (www.royal.gov.uk/ CharitiesandPatronages/Search Charities and Patronages.aspx).

The Queen also spends the evenings hosting state banquets or official receptions for diplomats, the Queen's Award for Industry or particular groups in the community including one for people from the British design and music worlds. The Queen also hosts receptions for guests who have a connection to her next incoming or outgoing state visit.

Pocket fact 📷

The Queen is never off duty and even on the wedding day of her grandson Prince William she had to leave the reception to meet with the prime minister of Australia, Julia Gillard.

♔ THE QUEEN'S HOBBIES ♔

Although the Queen's days are full of official duties she does also find time to indulge her private interests such as horse racing and the running of her estates of Windsor, Sandringham and Balmoral and its tenant farmers and employees in which she takes a close interest.

THE QUEEN'S HORSES

The Queen's love of horses started at a very early age. She was given her first pony Peggy at four years old. At the age of five the Queen began riding lessons and was taught by Owen, the groom at Royal Lodge, Windsor where the Royal Family was living at the time.

Pocket fact 📷

As children the Queen and her sister Margaret had over 30 toy horses that had to be unsaddled every night before they went to bed.

Horses meant freedom for the young princesses Elizabeth and Margaret, who otherwise had a very closeted existence. When staying up in Balmoral in Scotland with their parents, horses gave them freedom as they were allowed to ride their horses over the moors although a policeman did have to cycle behind them!

Pocket fact 🔟

The Queen always rides in a headscarf and not a traditional hard riding hat.

Riding astride a horse would not do for more official occasions such as Trooping the Colour and so the Queen had formal riding lessons to learn to ride side-saddle from Horace Smith, the royal riding instructor. The Queen also learnt to drive carriages and in 1944 she won the Single Private Driving on her pony Hans in the Royal Windsor Horse Show.

The Queen is also involved in horse racing and breeding, and the Royal Studs at Sandringham and Wolferton in Norfolk, Polhampton in Berkshire and the Royal Paddocks at Hampton Court have had an enormous amount of success. Today the Queen has about 25 horses in training and between 1988 and August 2011 her racing stables have had 330 winners and earned over £4m in prize money. The Queen's racing operation has to be self-funding as no money from the public purse can be used.

Top ten facts about the Queen and horse racing

1. *In 2011 the Queen's horse Carlton House was the favourite for the Epsom Derby. It came third.*
2. *The Queen has never won the Derby, the premier flat race in Britain. The closest the Queen's horses have come is second with Aureole in 1953.*
3. *The first royal horse the Queen saw win a race was Hypericum in 1946.*
4. *There is always a sweepstake held in the Royal Box for the Derby. In 2007 the Queen won with Authorized. The sweepstake is worth about £20.*

5. It is said by her racing manager John Warren that the Queen knows the condition of the racecourse at Royal Ascot by the sound her carriage wheels make on the course.

6. Every owner of a race horse has their own registered colours, the silk shirt and hat cover that the jockey wears. The Queen's colours are the ones used by George IV and Edward VII of a purple body with gold braid, scarlet sleeves and black velvet cap with gold fringe.

7. The Queen was the leading English horse breeder in her jubilee year in 1977.

8. In 1982, the Queen sold her broodmare Height of Fashion to Sheikh Hamdan al Maktoum for £1.25m, viewed as a colossal price at the time.

9. The Queen reads the Racing Post every day and has it sent to her electronically if she is abroad.

10. The Windsor Grey horses which pull the royal carriages are bred at Windsor and the Queen names them all herself, choosing from a list of places she has visited.

The Queen still rides today at the age of 85 and as recently as May 2011 pictures were published of her riding with two of her grandchildren. The Queen gave up riding for the Trooping the Colour in 1986 when her favourite mount Burmese retired (a gift from the Royal Canadian Mounted Police).

Pocket fact 🎲

The Queen was riding Burmese in 1981, when a man fired blanks from a replica gun at the Queen as the procession to the Trooping the Colour reached Horse Guards Parade. Burmese was startled but was soon brought under control by the Queen.

THE QUEEN'S DOGS

The Queen's love of dogs has been life-long and her corgis have become synonymous with the Queen herself. There are so many pictures of a small pack of dogs following her around and travelling with her and whenever possible the Queen looks after them herself. The dogs have their own bedroom and are exercised twice a day and fed three times a day.

Pocket fact 🎲

The Queen's dogs never eat tinned dog food. A footman brings the dogs' food of lamb, rabbit or beef, gravy, potatoes, cabbage and dog biscuits. The Queen remembers what every dog eats and mixes it herself.

The Queen's parents, George VI and Elizabeth, had a large selection of dogs when she was growing up including Labradors and Lhasa apsos. The long association of the Queen with corgis, a short-legged, bad-tempered Pembroke Welsh breed, started in 1933 when her father brought home a corgi called Rozavel Golden Eagle or Dookie.

Corgis

In 1944 when the Queen was 18 she was given her own corgi called Susan and many of the 30 corgis that the Queen has owned over the years are descended from Susan. Corgis are notoriously 'nippy' dogs and the Queen's corgis have bitten numerous members of the Queen's staff including the royal clock winder, a detective and a policeman.

The Queen introduced a new breed of dog when one of her corgis mated with one of Princess Margaret's dachshunds, Pipkin, resulting in a 'dorgi'. The Queen currently owns four corgis, Linnet, Monty, Willow and Holly, and three dorgis, Cider, Candy and Vulcan.

Pocket fact 🎲

When the corgi Susan died she was buried on the Sandringham Estate, as all the dogs are, with a small headstone designed by the Queen which said: 'Susan died 26 Jan 1959, for 15 years the faithful companion of the Queen.'

Gundogs

Although the abiding images of the Queen's dogs are of corgis, the Queen also breeds gundogs on the Sandringham Estate, Norfolk. The kennels were established by the Queen's great-grandfather King Edward VII in 1879. The kennels have around 25 dogs of varying ages and experience and include Labradors and cocker spaniels which are used by the Royal Family on shoots and provide the estate game keeper with working dogs. The Queen breeds prize-winning black Labradors and they have won five Field Trial Champions.

Pocket fact 🎲

The Queen once demoted a footman for giving one of the corgis whisky.

THE QUEEN'S PIGEONS

The Queen maintains a pigeon racing loft on the Sandringham Estate. In 1886 King Leopold of Belgium gave a gift of pigeons to the Royal Family. Both George V, the Queen's grandfather, and her uncle Edward VII won first prizes in the national race from Lerwick in the Shetland Isles. The Queen regularly visits the 160 mature pigeons, some kept for breeding and the others used for racing.

Pocket fact 🛈

The Queen is president of a number of pigeon racing societies, in particular The Royal Pigeon Racing Association and the National Flying Association.

The Sandringham pigeons are entered into club races each week and all national races during the racing season from April to September. The Queen's pigeon loft has been very successful over the years, winning every major race in the north and south of the UK.

♔ THE QUEEN ON TELEVISION ♔

The Royal Family (1969)

One of the overriding aspects of the Royal Family in the past was its mystique; no one was allowed to see them in their private moments and they guarded their private life jealously. In 1969 the Queen was the first monarch to allow their private life to become public as BBC television cameras filmed the Royal Family in their working and private life in a documentary called *The Royal Family*. The film showed the Queen as a wife and mother, chatting with her children and popping down to the local shop on the Balmoral Estate and buying sweets for the five-year-old Prince Edward.

The programme was broadcast on the BBC and two nights later on ITV. It caused a sensation as the public saw the Queen and the Royal Family sitting down to breakfast and Prince Philip barbecuing sausages on the Balmoral Estate. The programme was played over and over again and many thought it had completely destroyed the mystique of the monarchy and portrayed them as ordinary people. The video of the film is now unavailable as it was withdrawn in 1969 by the Royal Family and was never seen again until 2011 when the palace granted permission for the National Gallery to show 90-second clips of the film as part of its exhibition to celebrate the Queen's Diamond Jubilee.

Pocket fact 🖂

Princess Anne has said that she hated the documentary being made as they already spent so much of their life in the glare of the media that this was a step too far.

Elizabeth R (1992)

In 1992 the Queen decided again to let the cameras in and to celebrate the 40th anniversary of her accession to the throne. The BBC was allowed to film again but this time it focused mainly on her working life as a monarch. Narrated by the Queen and Ian Holm, the documentary is a wonderful insight into the working life of the Queen and the royal household. It shows the amount of work that goes into the planning of her regional visits and state visits where every aspect is planned to the minute and in detail and then discussed with the Queen so she knows exactly what is happening and when.

Pocket fact 🖂

The film shows one day where the Queen unveils four plaques, visits two town halls, launches one ship, opens one new bridge, one new bypass and visits one old people's home.

The documentary also shows the Queen during informal moments at the christening of Princess Eugenie, on holiday at Balmoral taking Princess Beatrice pony riding, and dancing at Balmoral looking relaxed, happy and laughing.

Royal remarks 🐕

The voiceover by the Queen reveals her thoughts on why she thinks she should visit the regions: 'Lots of people don't come to London very often so we travel to see them instead.'

The Queen's Castle (2004)

In 2004 the cameras documented life at Windsor Castle and the Windsor Estate. This film shows the state visit of the French President Jacques Chirac and the staging of the musical *Les Miserables* and the Order of the Garter Ceremony. There is extensive footage of Prince Philip in his role as Ranger of Windsor Park discussing plans for the park and the farm land. The documentary gives a real insight into the staff who work at the palace, including the timekeeper who takes 16 hours to adjust the clocks for British Summer Time.

Pocket fact 🚹

The documentary shows the Queen checking the table before the state banquet to ensure everything is correct.

The Queen at 80 (2006)

The BBC made a documentary to celebrate the 80th birthday of the Queen, charting her life using previously unseen and private footage of her wedding and coronation and her more troubled times following the death of Diana, Princess of Wales. The documentary includes interviews with British prime ministers Tony Blair, John Major and Edward Heath, where they discuss the advantages of being able to speak to someone in complete privacy who has a wide understanding and experience of current affairs. The programme also showed interviews with people who had received awards from the Queen and attended garden parties and what these meant to them.

The Monarchy: The Royal Family At Work (2007)

In 2007 the BBC and RDF Media followed the Queen for a year and provided a great insight into the role of the Queen as Head of State and Head of the Nation. The documentary shows her in the United States on a state visit and entertaining the President of Ghana at a state banquet at Buckingham Palace. The documentary also shows the work behind the garden parties, investitures and the State Opening of Parliament and stories from the public and world leaders including Tony Blair and President George W Bush.

♔ THE QUEEN IN FILM ♔

The Queen (2006)

This film deals with the time just after the death of Diana, Princess of Wales in 1997 and the monarchy's growing disconnection from the British public over their lack of reaction to the death of Diana. The film is a mixture of factual events, such as Tony Blair's speech when he refers to Diana as 'the people's princess' and the Queen and royal family walking among the flowers outside Buckingham Palace. The film received critical acclaim and won an Oscar for its star Helen Mirren, who played the Queen.

Pocket fact 🗟

The Queen's press secretary was asked if the Queen liked the film and she replied that the Queen would never comment on what she did or didn't like as it would be like advertising and the Queen never endorses a product.

The King's Speech (2010)

This film is based on the true story of the Queen's father George VI's struggle with his stammer and the help given by Lionel Logue, an Australian speech therapist. The film begins in 1936 when George VI becomes king after his brother Edward VIII abdicated the throne to marry Wallis Simpson (see p.4). The film shows how George VI overcame his stammer and made a radio broadcast at the beginning of the war that united and inspired the people. The film also gives an insight into the people the Queen's father and mother were and her early family life.

♔ THE QUEEN'S PORTRAITS ♔

The Queen is probably the most visually represented person in the world with official photographs taken to celebrate her birthdays, coronation, anniversaries, the births of her children and jubilees. The Queen had her first official photograph taken in May 1926 when she was just a month old at her christening at Buckingham Palace. In the early part of her reign the portraits, whether photographs or paintings, continued with the traditional image of the monarch portrayed in all their pomp and ceremony.

As the Queen's reign progressed more informal and natural portraits started to appear like those taken in 1978 to celebrate her 52nd birthday, showing her holding her grandson Peter Phillips.

The Queen has had numerous portraits painted for many different organisations including one for the shipping company Cunard for their latest cruise ship, the *Queen Elizabeth*, painted by Isobel Peachey. The Queen's portrait has been painted by a number of artists from the famous Pietro Annigoni portrait in 1956 which captured a beautiful young woman in her garter robes (see p.96) to the controversial portrait by Lucien Freud in 2001, which the editor of the *British Art Journal* was quoted as saying it made her 'look like one of the corgis who has suffered a stroke'.

Pocket fact 🎗

On the National Portrait Gallery website there are 451 portraits associated with the Queen.

Photographs of the Queen have been taken by famous photographers including Lord Snowdon, Cecil Beaton and Lord Lichfield. More recently the photographers have been Jane Brown, who took the Queen's 80th birthday portrait, and Annie Lebovitz, who took her photograph in 2007, just before the Queen's six-day tour of America.

Pocket fact 🔋

The most unusual portrait of the Queen is the hologram called 'The Lightness of Being', created by Chris Levine for the Island of Jersey to celebrate 800 years of loyalty to the English Crown. Chris Levine took over 10,000 images of the Queen and three-dimensional images during two sittings at Buckingham Palace.